ELECTROCULTURE BIBLE

[7-IN-1] The Complete Guide to Growing High-Yield Crops and Improving Soil Health Without Chemical Inputs | Boost Your Plant Growth by 300% with the Power of Electricity

Rick Croppield

RICK CROPPIELD © Copyright 2023. All Rights Reserved.

The publication is sold with the idea that the publisher is not required to render accounting, officially permitted or otherwise qualified services. This document is geared towards providing exact and reliable information concerning the topic and issue covered. If advice is necessary, legal or professional, a practiced individual in the profession should be ordered.

- From a Declaration of Principles which was accepted and approved equally by a Committee of the American Bar Association and a Committee of Publishers and Associations.

In no way is it legal to reproduce, duplicate, or transmit any part of this document in either electronic means or printed format. Recording of this publication is strictly prohibited, and any storage of this document is not allowed unless with written permission from the publisher—all rights reserved.

The information provided herein is stated to be truthful and consistent. Any liability, in terms of inattention or otherwise, by any usage or abuse of any policies, processes, or directions contained within is the sole and utter responsibility of the recipient reader. Under no circumstances will any legal responsibility or blame be held against the publisher for any reparation, damages, or monetary loss due to the information herein, either directly or indirectly.

Respective authors own all copyrights not held by the publisher.

The information herein is offered for informational purposes solely and is universal as so. The presentation of the information is without a contract or any guarantee assurance.

The trademarks that are used are without any consent, and the publication of the trademark is without permission or backing by the trademark owner. All trademarks and brands within this book are for clarifying purposes only and are owned by the owners themselves, not affiliated with this document.

TABLE OF CONTENTS

PART 1 5
- BRIEF HISTORY OF ELECTROCULTURE 7
- THEORETICAL FOUNDATIONS OF ELECTROCULTURE 7
- BENEFITS AND DRAWBACKS OF ELECTROCULTURE 8

PART 2: THE SCIENCE OF ELECTROCULTURE 14
- PLANT PHYSIOLOGY AND ELECTROCHEMISTRY 14
- ELECTRICAL PROPERTIES OF PLANTS 20
- MECHANISMS OF ACTION OF ELECTROCULTURE ON PLANTS 25

PART 3: ELECTRODES AND POWER SUPPLIES 31
- TYPES OF ELECTRODES USED IN ELECTROCULTURE 31
- POWER SOURCES FOR ELECTROCULTURE 34
- METHODS FOR MEASURING ELECTRICAL CURRENT AND VOLTAGE 40

PART 4: APPLICATIONS OF ELECTROCULTURE 45
- ELECTROCULTURE IN AGRICULTURE 45
- ELECTROCULTURE IN HORTICULTURE 52
- ELECTROCULTURE IN VITICULTURE 58
- ELECTROCULTURE IN AQUAPONICS AND HYDROPONICS 62
- ELECTROCULTURE IN FORESTRY 67

PART 5: BENEFITS AND CHALLENGES OF ELECTROCULTURE 73
- IMPROVED PLANT GROWTH AND YIELDS 73
- REDUCED NEED FOR FERTILIZERS AND PESTICIDES 74
- IMPROVED SOIL HEALTH 75
- POTENTIAL FOR GREENHOUSE GAS REDUCTION 76
- SAFETY CONCERNS OF ELECTROCULTURE 77
- CONTROVERSIES AND SKEPTICISM 78
- TECHNICAL AND ECONOMIC CHALLENGES 79

PART 6: FUTURE DIRECTIONS IN ELECTROCULTURE 80
- RESEARCH NEEDS AND OPPORTUNITIES 80
- TECHNOLOGICAL DEVELOPMENTS 81
- POLICY IMPLICATIONS OF ELECTROCULTURE 85
- FUTURE TRENDS IN ELECTROCULTURE 94

PART 7: PRACTICAL ASPECTS OF ELECTROCULTURE 99

- **IMPLEMENTING ELECTROCULTURE IN PRACTICE** 102
- **BEST PRACTICES FOR ELECTROCULTURE** 104
- **COST-BENEFIT ANALYSIS OF ELECTROCULTURE** 106

CONCLUSION *116*

PART 1

When you apply electricity, magnetism, monochrome light, and sound to plants, it can make them grow. This new technology, known as Electroculture, has successfully helped gardeners increase their plants' growth rates, increase yields, and produce quality crops. It also protects plants from diseases, insects, and frost. Fortunately, you will need less fertilizer or pesticides. Henceforth, Farmers will grow bigger and better crops within a short period, efficiently, effectively, and affordably.

Electroculture gardening is easy and does not require special equipment or training to begin using. All you need are some basic tools and materials including knowledge about electricity to start creating an electroculture setup tailored specifically to the needs of your plants and garden. So how does electroculture gardening work? You just have to put plants in a weak electrical field or current to help them grow. You can do these from the options below:

- **Direct current (DC) stimulation**: This occurs when you add a small amount of direct current (DC) electricity directly to the plant or soil. The current is made from a battery or low-voltage power source and transferred to the plant by burying electrodes or coiling cables around it.

- **Alternating current (AC) stimulation**: This occurs when you add a weak AC electric field around the soil or plant. You bury wires or electrodes in the soil or wrap them around the plant to make the field, which is often made with an AC power source or a special electroculture device.

- **Induction stimulation**: This occurs when you use special electroculture equipment to create a low-level AC electric field in the soil or plant tissue. The machine makes an electromagnetic field without using wires or electrodes. This field enables plants to grow and develop.

Electroculture gardening, irrespective of the method used, is to create an electrical environment that enables plants to grow and develop. Just thoroughly control the electrical stimulation's voltage, current, and frequency, including its length and timing.

Although electroculture gardening is a new method of cultivating plants, several studies have already proven its effectiveness. Recent studies have proven that electroculture can help plants such as tomatoes, peppers, lettuce, and strawberries to grow and yield more.

It also helps plants to absorb nutrients and their mineral content. This enables fruits and vegetables that are healthier to gain more nutrients. So, how can you get started with electroculture gardening? Below are some tips:

- **Do your homework**: Before you start, do more research about electroculture gardening. Search for forums, blogs, and articles on the internet that teaches you everything needed to get started with electroculture gardening.

- **Select your method**: As mentioned earlier, there are several ways to do electroculture gardening. Consider your garden space and the plants you want to grow to determine which method will suit you.

- **Collect your supplies**: A few basic items will help you get started with ElectroCulture gardening. For instance, using DC stimulation requires electrodes or wires and a battery or a source of low-voltage power. Also, using AC stimulation requires wires or electrodes and an AC power supply or electroculture device.

- **Start small**: As a newbie to electroculture gardening, it's best to start small and experiment with a few plants or a small area of your garden. This helps you to get an idea of the process and improve your strategy before considering a bigger garden.

As part of your experiment with electroculture gardening, observe your plants closely and write down all observations regarding voltage, current, and frequency stimulation as well as exposure time duration and duration. Doing this will allow you to continuously refine what and how you are doing things. This will lead to improved results both in terms of results and methodology.

Electroculture gardening offers a novel and exciting method of cultivating plants that may lead to higher crop yields, higher quality harvests, and decreased fertilizer and chemical needs. When applying electrical stimulation within gardening techniques, you provide optimal conditions for healthy plant development for stronger and more productive results. Anyone can try electroculture gardening and reap its benefits with a little research, experimentation, and attention to detail.

BRIEF HISTORY OF ELECTROCULTURE

As mentioned earlier, electroculture is a fairly new concept that uses electricity to grow plants faster and yield more crops. This concept was stated in the 18th century when an Italian scientist named Luigi Galvani discovered that animals have bio-electricity. However, electroculture became popular in enhancing agricultural production in the 20th century.

At the beginning of the 20th century, a French engineer known as Paul Divry started testing how electricity influenced plant growth. He learned that running electrical currents through the soil boosted plant growth and increased crop yields. During that time, scientists disregarded Divry's work, yet other scientists decided to consider the potential of electroculture.

In the 1930s, Soviet scientist V. Chizhevsky also carried out tests to understand how electrical fields influenced the plant's growth. He learned that plants subjected to high-frequency electrical fields grew faster and suffered less illness. Thereafter, other Soviet scientists built on Chizhevsky's work and discovered several ways to boost crop yields using electroculture.

In the United States, electroculture became renowned in the 1950s and 1960s, particularly among hobbyists and people who cultivated plants in their backyards. Several of these electroculture fans made their own devices at home and revealed amazing results. Unfortunately, commercial farmers never adopted electroculture, and several people disregarded it in the second half of the 20th century.

Nowadays, electroculture remains a small field. Only a few researchers and farmers are discovering its benefits in farming. As more people become concerned with food security and sustainable farming methods, electroculture could become increasingly popular over time.

THEORETICAL FOUNDATIONS OF ELECTROCULTURE

Electroculture is founded upon scientific principles of electrochemistry, electromagnetism, and plant physiology.

Electrochemistry

Electrochemistry is vital to electroculture as it explains how electrical currents can alter chemical reactions within soil and plant tissues. When an electric current is run through the soil, several chemical reactions that can affect plant growth occur. For example, electric currents enable nutrients in the soil to become soluble for plant roots to reach. This enables plants to take in nutrients and grow.

Electromagnetism

Electromagnetism plays an integral part in electroculture; plants respond to electromagnetic fields which influence how they grow and change over time. People who practice electroculture experience faster plant growth and more crops from them by creating an electromagnetic environment. Just use electric currents to create magnetic fields or permanent magnets to create a static magnetic field. These magnetic fields can change how plant cells are structured and enable them to absorb nutrients.

Physiology

Plant physiology is also relevant to electroculture. Electrical currents enable plant growth by changing physiological processes like cell division, nutrient uptake, and hormone production. Electrical stimulation helps plants to produce more plant hormones, such as auxins and gibberellins, which control how plants grow and develop. Henceforth, electroculture fans can increase plant growth and crop yields.

In conclusion, electroculture is based on the theories of electrochemistry, electromagnetism, and plant physiology. Electroculture boosts crop yields and plant growth through electrical currents and magnetic fields to change the chemical and physiological processes occurring in plants and soil. Although more research is needed to grasp electroculture, it is a relevant tool for sustainable agriculture.

BENEFITS AND DRAWBACKS OF ELECTROCULTURE

Benefits

Here is a detailed list of benefits of electroculture:

- Increasing crop yields: Studies have proven that electroculture can increase crop yields by up to 200%. Electrical currents enable plants to get bigger and yield more fruits, flowers, or seeds.

- Reduced water use: Electroculture enables plants to absorb water more efficiently. Therefore, irrigation won't require plenty of water. This benefit will favor places where water is scarce.

- Reduced fertilizer and pesticide use: Electroculture produces healthier and stronger plants, so fewer fertilizers and pesticides will be used. Therefore, this reduces the costs and damage that traditional farming does to the environment.

- Increased nutrient uptake: Electroculture usually increases nutrient uptake from the soil, such as nitrogen, phosphate, and potassium. This enables plants and crops to get stronger and be good for consumption.

- Better soil health: Electroculture's use of low-level electrical currents gives room for beneficial microbes, such as mycorrhizal fungi and nitrogen-fixing bacteria, to develop in the soil. This enables a healthier and more fertile soil that absorbs water and air.

- Improved plant resistance: Electroculture enables plants to be more resistant to factors such as heat, cold, and drought. Therefore, plants become stronger to cope with environmental changes.

- Faster plant growth: Electroculture uses electrical currents that increase cell division and growth for plants to grow faster and reduce their growing seasons. Places, where the growing season is short, will reap this benefit.

- Enhanced crop quality: Electroculture gives crops a sweet taste, feel, and more nutrients. Therefore quality crops produced can be sold for more money on the market.

- Reduced plant disease: Electroculture uses electrical currents to prevent or reduce plant disease because they motivate plants to develop their natural defenses.

- Less reliance on fossil fuels: Electroculture reduces the value of synthetic fertilizers and pesticides to reduce the use of fossil fuels in conventional agriculture.

- Lower production costs: Electroculture is an alternative for farmers with water scarcity; therefore, fertilizer and pesticides with electroculture production costs are reduced.
- Sustainable agriculture: Electroculture is a sustainable farming method that minimizes the damage that farming does to the environment. It enhances soil health, uses less water, and minimizes the use of synthetic inputs.

- Improved biodiversity: Since electroculture enhances soil health and minimizes the use of synthetic inputs, it can improve biodiversity by creating a more diverse and healthy ecosystem.

- Increased food security: Since electroculture boosts crop yields and enhances crop quality, it can increase food security, particularly in areas with few agricultural resources.

- Better seed germination: Electroculture uses electric currents that help seeds sprout and grow into healthy seedlings.

- Improved root growth: Electroculture makes roots grow faster to produce stronger and more resilient plants that can absorb nutrients.

- Reduced soil erosion: Since electroculture enhances soil health, it also minimizes soil erosion and creates stable soil.

- Reduced greenhouse gas emissions: Electroculture uses fewer synthetic inputs to minimize the greenhouse gas emissions from producing and transporting these synthetic inputs.

- Organic farming is supported: Electroculture complies with organic agricultural principles. Therefore, you can easily use natural fertilizers and pesticides and reduce the need for chemicals.

- Production on a large scale: Electroculture can be applied on a large scale as a promising strategy for sustainable agriculture for farmers globally.

In summary, electroculture is an innovative technology with several advantages for agriculture and the environment. It supports farmers to use practices that are good for the environment, minimizes the damage farming does to the environment, and increases crop yields and quality. With time, research on electroculture might be an important tool for farmers seeking to boost yields and reduce environmental impact.

Drawbacks

Electroculture provides many advantages to agriculture and the environment, but there are certain drawbacks and limitations attached to its implementation. Below are some of these:

- High initial cost: Electroculture equipment can be expensive, which might deter farmers, particularly small-scale ones, from using it.

- Needs specialized training: Electroculture needs specialized training due to the technicalities involved. Unfortunately, this can be difficult for farmers because they might lack the required training.

- Limited research: Little research is carried out on the long-term effects of electroculture on soil health and crop productivity, which will reduce the knowledge and reliability of electroculture.

- Lack of standardization: Currently, there are no standards for electroculture equipment or its usage, which can create different results and make it difficult to compare studies.

- Electric shock risk: The use of electricity in electroculture gives room for getting an electric shock, which can be fatal.

- Failure of equipment: Just like any piece of equipment, there is always a chance of failure, which can cause crop loss or environmental damage.

- Needs regular maintenance: The equipment used in electroculture needs regular maintenance to ensure effective performance and safety.

- Requires a power source: Electroculture uses a power source, which can be difficult for farmers in remote or off-grid areas.

- Limited use: The benefits of electroculture may not work for all crops or growing conditions, which can be inapplicable for some farmers.

- Scalability issues: The equipment used in electroculture may not be useful on a large scale, which can be inapplicable for larger farms.

- Possible damage to the environment: The use of electricity in electroculture could damage the environment if the technology is wrongly used.

- Possibility for negative effects on soil health: While electroculture has been demonstrated to promote soil health in some circumstances, the electrical currents employed in electroculture might damage soil microbes and nutrient availability.

- Reduced effectiveness in extreme conditions: Electroculture may be limited in extreme conditions, including drought, flood, or extreme heat.

- Limitations in some types of soil: The benefits of electroculture may be limited in some types of soil, especially those with a lot of clay or little organic matter.

- Limitations in some places: Electroculture may be limited in some places because of differences in soil, climate, or growing conditions.

- Limited availability: The equipment and technology needed for electroculture may be scarce in developing countries or rural areas.

- Inadequate support: Farmers might not get the help and materials required to successfully use electroculture.

- Adoption may be limited: Although electroculture has several benefits, there may be limited usage because of the challenges and limits discussed above.

- Possible unintended consequences: Using electroculture may have unintended effects that we are yet to grasp, particularly in the long run.

- Concerns about ethics: Some people may have ethical concerns about electroculture and its effect on the environment and the well-being of animals.

In conclusion, electroculture could enhance agriculture and the environment in several ways, but it also has some problems that need to be considered. Just like any new technology, it should be carefully adopted and used to ensure safety, usefulness, and durability.

PART 2: THE SCIENCE OF ELECTROCULTURE

PLANT PHYSIOLOGY AND ELECTROCHEMISTRY

Plant physiology shows how plants work and respond to their environment. This involves their growth process, reproduction, and use of energy. However, electrochemistry talks about chemical reactions whereby electrons move from one species to another. When plant physiology and electrochemistry merge, you'll understand how plants use and respond to electrical signals, including those used in photosynthesis and respiration.

The study of plant physiology and electrochemistry is relevant in discovering how plants respond to things like climate change and how we can develop more sustainable methods to farm. This section explains how plant physiology and electrochemistry are related and shows the relevance of this field of study.

PLANT PHYSIOLOGY

As mentioned earlier, plant physiology is the scientific method that shows how plants work and respond to their surroundings. It explains what goes on inside plant cells, tissues, and organs and how they work.

Processes and functions studied in Plant Physiology

Plant physiology involves several processes and functions, such as photosynthesis, respiration, absorbing and moving water, absorbing and spreading nutrients, growing and developing, and reproducing. All these things determine the growth, development, and reproduction of plants and help plants to live.

Plants adopt light energy to convert carbon dioxide and water into glucose and oxygen, which is known as photosynthesis. The process of respiration shows how plants break down glucose to get energy for their cells. For the plant to access water and nutrients to all of its parts, it needs to absorb and move water. Nutrient acquisition and distribution show how important elements like nitrogen and phosphorus are absorbed and moved around the plant.

As a plant gets older, it experiences several physical and chemical changes, such as creating new tissues and organs. These changes are known as growth and development. Plants reproduce by making seeds, flowers, and fruit, all of which make the species survive.

Importance of Plant Physiology in Agriculture and Medicine

Research on plant physiology is useful in several ways in agriculture and medicine. Understanding how plants function on a physiological level can enable us to create new plant varieties with greater resistance against pests and diseases, can better handle environmental stresses like drought or extreme temperatures, and produce greater crops.

Research in plant physiology has also led to the creation of new medicines derived from plant compounds. Medicines such as aspirin and taxol derived from plants help treat various illnesses like cancer, cardiovascular disease, and inflammation.

Plant physiology enables one to understand how plants function in response to their environment and can be applied in agriculture, medicine, and protecting the environment, as well as developing technologies and strategies for feeding an ever-increasing global population while conserving natural resources.

ELECTROCHEMISTRY

Electrochemistry is a field of chemistry that investigates how electricity affects chemical reactions. Electrons move from one chemical species to another during these reactions, producing new chemical compounds or altering existing ones in ways that alter their properties.

How electricity and chemical reactions work together

A process called electrolysis shows the relationship between electricity and chemical reactions. Electrolysis involves using an electric current to trigger chemical reactions that would not normally take place on their own, thus converting electric energy to chemical energy and vice versa. Moreover, electrochemistry explores electrochemical cells, which are devices that make electricity from chemical reactions that occur independently.

Applications of electrochemistry in science and industry

Electrochemistry has many practical applications in science and business. Batteries, which consist of electrochemical cells that store and release electricity, are one common example. Batteries can power portable electronics as well as run electric cars.

Electrochemistry has many applications beyond metal production and other chemical production. One such use of electroplating involves depositing thin layers of metal onto surfaces using electric current. This process gives jewelry and other metal objects decorative finishes and ensures that metal parts are immune to rust.

Electrochemistry is also used in the field of analytical chemistry to discover how much of a specific chemical is in a sample. Electrochemical sensors can discover several analytes, such as glucose, cholesterol, and various gasses.

In conclusion, electrochemistry is relevant in many parts of modern life, from storing energy to studying materials to monitoring the environment.

ELECTROCHEMISTRY IN PLANT PHYSIOLOGY

Importance of electrochemistry in studying plant physiology

Electrochemistry is an integral component of studying plant physiology as it provides researchers with an opportunity to uncover how electrochemical processes take place within plant cells. Researchers can assess and measure the electrical properties of plant tissues with these techniques. This can help them discover how different physiological processes work.

Examples of electrochemical techniques used in plant physiology

Patch clamping is one type of electrochemical technique used in plant physiology. Patch clamping helps to measure the electrical activity of individual ion channels in a plant cell membrane through a tiny glass electrode. Researchers can utilize this technique to gain insight into how ion channels function and their effect on cellular processes such as the movement of nutrients and water, signaling pathways, and other processes.

Electrochemical impedance spectroscopy (EIS) is another technique utilized in plant physiology that utilizes electricity. EIS involves administering small AC voltage to plant tissue and measuring any changes to an electrical impedance that occur as time progresses. Researchers can utilize EIS to measure the physical and chemical properties of plant tissues, including their membrane permeability, the water content in tissue volumes, and how well it transports ions across it.

Role of electrochemistry in understanding photosynthesis and respiration

Electrochemistry is also relevant in understanding how plants do photosynthesis and respiration. Photosynthesis occurs when light energy is converted into chemical energy. This energy creates glucose and other organic molecules. Researchers can study how electrons move, and energy is transferred during photosynthesis through electrochemical measurements.

Similarly, respiration includes breaking down organic molecules to release energy for plants to power various cellular processes. Electrochemical techniques allow us to study the electron transfer activities that take place during respiration and their results in pH and ion concentration changes, as well as measure their effects.

Electrochemistry can be a useful method of investigating plant physiology as it provides a means of measuring and analyzing electrochemical processes occurring within plant cells. We understand how photosynthesis and respiration work through electrochemical techniques. These techniques could also help us understand how other physiological processes work.

FUTURE DIRECTIONS

Emerging trends in the study of Plant Physiology and Electrochemistry

- Plant-Microbial Interactions: Recent research has emphasized the significance of plant-microbial interactions for nutrient uptake, plant growth, and disease resistance. Plant physiology and electrochemistry provide valuable tools to understand these interactions more fully.

- Nanotechnology: Nanotechnology is an emerging area in plant sciences. Researchers are investigating how nanomaterials could assist plant growth while relieving stress more effectively.

- Plant Electrophysiology: Electrophysiology is the study of electrical properties found within living cells and tissues. An emerging field in plant electrophysiology seeks to discover how plants use electrical signals as means of communicating between themselves and their surroundings.

- Plant Stress Physiology: With climate change taking hold, it has become important to study how plants respond to stress. Researchers are investigating physiological and electrochemical changes experienced during periods of high stress to discover ways to make stronger plants.

Potential applications of Plant Physiology and Electrochemistry in Agriculture and Medicine

- Crop Improvement: Understanding the physiology and electrochemistry of plants can help create crops more resistant to pests, diseases, and environmental stressors - helping increase crop yields while providing enough food for all.

- Production of Bioenergy: Plant physiology and electrochemistry can assist with creating eco-friendly bioenergy production systems such as those for producing biofuels and biogas that provide sustainable solutions.

- Plant-Based Medicines: Plants contain many compounds with medicinal uses, so understanding their physiology and electrochemistry may lead to new plant-based medications being discovered.

- Monitoring the Environment: Since plants are highly responsive to changes in their environments, studying their physiology and electrochemistry can give us insight into their quality and level of pollution.

Challenges and opportunities in the field

- Improvements in Technology: Plant physiology and electrochemistry fields continue to change rapidly as new technologies appear, creating both challenges and opportunities. Adjusting to these changes may be challenging but can open many doors of opportunity.

- Interdisciplinary Cooperation: Both plant physiology and electrochemistry require expertise in several different disciplines, including biology, chemistry, and physics. As experts from these respective fields come together, their collaboration will advance both fields.
- Data Analysis and Interpretation: Plant physiology and electrochemistry produce copious amounts of data that are often difficult to evaluate or interpret, creating challenges when trying to make sense of these complex data sets. To make our work meaningful we must find new approaches for interpreting it.

- Funding and Support: Plant physiology and electrochemistry research require significant financial investment from institutions; researchers in developing countries may find it more challenging to access such support; however, investments made now could greatly benefit agriculture and medicine in the long term.

Plant physiology and electrochemistry are closely intertwined fields of study that benefit agriculture, medicine, and environmental health. Plant physiology studies how plants function while electrochemistry explores electricity and chemical reactions between living cells in plants - when combined researchers can study electrical properties within living tissues that help understand plant growth, stress relief strategies, or illness prevention.

Plant physiology and electrochemistry research offer many promising opportunities shortly, such as creating environmentally resilient crops, developing innovative medicines from plants, or using plants as bioenergy sources. Yet researchers must face difficulties such as keeping pace with advances in technology while finding funding support for their work.

Plant physiology and electrochemistry studies can provide valuable solutions to some of the tough problems facing agriculture, medicine, and the environment. More research in these fields will allow us to discover what plants can offer us while supporting life on Earth.

ELECTRICAL PROPERTIES OF PLANTS

Electrical properties refer to how plants generate, transmit, and use electric signals including their ability to send or receive them which plays an integral part in biological processes like growth and development, or reacting to things in their environment. Understanding how plants use electricity can provide us with insights into plant activities while opening up possibilities for crop management or farming practices.

ELECTROLYTE CONDUCTIVITY

Electrolyte conductivity refers to the ability of an electrolyte solution to conduct electricity. An electrolyte is defined as any substance which ionizes when mixed with solvent, producing charged particles known as ions that conduct electricity when exposed to electricity. An electric field applied to an electrolyte solution causes its ions to move towards opposite electrodes, creating an electrical current. The conductivity of an electrolyte solution depends on both the concentration and mobility of its ions. Temperature, pressure, and the presence of impurities all play an integral part in electrolyte conductivity. Electrolyte conductivity has wide-reaching significance across chemistry, biology, and electrochemistry fields; batteries, fuel cells, and sensors all use electrolytes with different conductivities to function optimally.

Importance of Electrolyte Conductivity in plants

Electrolyte conductivity is vitally important to plants as it plays an integral part in their ability to transport nutrients and water. Electric charges flowing through a plant's cells allow water and dissolved nutrients from the soil into its leaves or other parts. The rate at which this happens depends upon concentrations of ions within its tissues as well as the conductivity of its cell membranes.

Electrolyte conductivity plays an essential role in maintaining plant water balance. Under stress caused by drought, salinity, or extreme temperatures, electrolyte imbalance may occur and result in altered cell conductivity - disrupting its ability to absorb water and nutrients from its soil and transport them throughout its body.

Electrolyte conductivity not only regulates water balance in plants, but it can also play an integral part in responding to environmental stressors. For instance, plants exposed to high salt concentrations may face changes in their electrolyte balance that produce protective compounds and proteins for coping with stress.

In conclusion, electrolyte conductivity is a relevant physiological process in plants that affects the plant's ability to maintain water and nutrient balance, respond to environmental stress, and eventually grow and develop well.

Examples of Electrolyte Conductivity in plants

Potassium ions moving across the cell membrane is one of the common examples of how electrolytes move through plants. This movement is useful for a plant's water balance because it maintains the turgor pressure of its cells steady. The movement of calcium ions is another example. Calcium ions play an essential role in plant development and growth.

ACTION POTENTIALS

Action potentials, also known as transient shifts of the cell membrane's electrical potential that result from external stimuli, occur quickly when exposed to stimuli like moving ions across its membrane. Plant cells experience this type of action potential when their electrical potential changes quickly in response to external stimulation.

Importance of Action Potentials in Plants

Action potentials serve a critical function in plants: communication and signaling between different parts. One primary use for action potentials in plants is moving electrical signals from roots to leaves, helping plants quickly react to environmental changes like temperature shifts, light patterns, or moisture changes - for instance, if moisture levels suddenly decrease, an action potential might travel from roots to leaves to close stomata and prevent any further water loss.

Action potentials play an essential role in plant development and growth, regulating various physiological processes that involve opening and closing stomata, the movement of nutrients and water throughout a plant's system, and even root development and shoot growth.

Recent research suggests that action potentials may also help plants react to external stimuli like insect damage or pathogen attack, prompting an action potential that travels throughout the plant's cells and produces defensive compounds to stop further damage.

In conclusion, action potentials play a vital role in plant life. They facilitate communication and signaling between different parts of a plant's anatomy, regulate physiological processes and respond to environmental stimuli.

Examples of Action Potentials in Plants

Venus Flytraps are one of the more commonly-known plants with action potentials; when an insect lands on one of its leaves, an action potential occurs, and its leaves close around it to trap it. They also respond when touched; for instance, Mimosa plants also react this way.

MEMBRANE POTENTIAL

Membrane potential refers to the difference between electrical potentials inside and outside a cell membrane. As ions move across its surfaces, creating membrane potential.

Importance of Membrane Potential in Plants

Membrane potential plays an essential role in numerous physiological processes, including nutrient uptake, water transport, and signal transduction. One key function of membrane potential in plants is absorbing essential nutrients like potassium and calcium via the electrochemical gradient created by membrane potential; their absorption facilitates plant growth and development while helping regulate concentrations within plant cells.

Membrane potential also plays a key role in water movement throughout a plant. Water moves from areas with higher water potential to those with lower potential; and membrane potential helps maintain this gradient across plant cells to regulate absorption and loss, an essential factor for plant survival.

Membrane potential plays an essential role in signal transduction for plants. Several signaling pathways in plants rely on changes to membrane potential that enable or disable various ion channels and pumps - helping plants respond rapidly to changing environmental factors like light intensity, temperature, or the presence of pathogens.

As stated before, membrane potential plays an essential role in plant physiology by regulating essential processes like nutrient absorption, water transport, and signal transduction. Gaining insight into this aspect of plant biology enables us to create strategies to increase plant growth and productivity and advance knowledge.

Examples of Membrane Potential in Plants

Plants utilize membrane potential by controlling when their stomata open and close. If needed to conserve water, plants use membrane potential changes of guard cells to close stomata by altering their membrane potential - similar changes occur with root hair growth, too! Changing membrane potential also impacts how quickly hair grows back on roots.

CAPACITANCE

Plant capacitance refers to the ability of cell membranes or structures within cells to store an electric charge. Capacitance plays an integral part in many physiological processes, including signal transduction between cells as well as the movement of ions across membranes and fluid across cell boundaries. Electrical charges stored in plant cells can be measured through patch-clamp recordings or impedance spectroscopy techniques.

Importance of Capacitance in Plants

Capacitance plays an essential role in many physiological processes in plants. One such process is transpiration - moving water molecules from roots to leaves through small openings known as stomata on leaves - allowing transpiration. Capacitance also allows plants to save water in their tissues to maintain turgor pressure - the force that keeps plants upright.

Capacitance plays an integral role in photosynthesis. Photosynthesis occurs when plants convert sunlight to chemical energy in the form of glucose. Plants absorb light energy that they store as electrical charge in capacitance storage; later on, this energy can power several cellular processes within their plants.

Capacitance also assists plants with regulating ion transport in plants, which allows for physiological processes like osmotic regulation, enzyme activation, and nutrient uptake. Through capacitance, the plant can control how many ions move across cell membranes to ensure balance and overall plant health.

Capacitance plays an integral role in many physiological processes of plants, such as water transport, photosynthesis, and ion regulation.

Example of Capacitance in Plants

Capacitance shows how plant cells can store electrical energy while action potentials are being created, or during photosynthesis when energy can be stored up and used to form ATP.

BIOPHOTON EMISSION

Biophoton Emission in Plants Photon emission occurs as part of several biological processes in plants, including photosynthesis, respiration, and oxidative metabolism. The phenomenon has been widely researched, as evidenced by its ability to control plant growth and development as well as help them adapt to their surroundings.

Biophoton emission from plants occurs as the result of reactive oxygen species (ROS) created during photosynthesis and respiration, communicating with chromophores within cells to create photon emission. Light intensity, temperature, and availability of water all play an important part in how much biophoton emission there is in plants.

Research in plant biophoton emission has led to several non-invasive methods for tracking plant growth and stress responses, such as measuring biophoton emission to evaluate seed quality, identify early signs of plant disease, or monitor how drought or pollution stressors impact plant health.

Importance of Biophoton Emission in Plants

Biophoton emission plays a crucial role in photosynthesis using light energy. Plants use photosynthesis to convert carbon dioxide and water into glucose and oxygen for vitality and survival. Biophoton emissions regulate this process by providing feedback about the availability and quality of light sources to plants.

Biophoton emission also plays a vital role in helping plants to develop and grow. According to studies, plants emitting more biophotons during times of rapid development is suggestive of their internal clock having controlled this process.

Biophoton emission also allows plants to communicate. Plants emit biophotons when responding to different stimuli such as temperature shifts or predator presence; these emissions serve as signals to nearby plants that help them adapt quickly to changes in their environments or identify threats more easily.

In sum, Biophoton emission in plants is highly important. It helps regulate photosynthesis, growth, and communication processes while learning more about it could provide new insight into how they function within their ecosystems.

Example of Biophoton Emission in Plants

Biophotons can be produced when plants produce light during photosynthesis or action potentials cause cells to emit light as a measurement of electrically active plant cells.

Conclusion

Electrolyte conductivity, action potentials, membrane potential capacitance, and biophoton emission are some of the electrical properties found in plants that allow them to grow, develop and respond appropriately in their environment.

Learning how plants utilize electricity can teach us much about how plants work and help us find new methods of farming and crop management. Furthermore, studying their use can reveal diseases prevalent within plants that need to be prevented from spreading further; finally, it may even aid us in creating drugs and treatments to combat human illnesses.

MECHANISMS OF ACTION OF ELECTROCULTURE ON PLANTS

The following are the mechanisms of action of electroculture on plants:

Electrochemical effects

- Ionization of nutrients: Applying electrical currents through the soil can ionize nutrients for plants to absorb. Such treatments may enhance plant growth and increase yields in soils with limited nutrients.

- Increase in pH level: Electroculture can also change the pH level of the soil to create more alkaline. This can make more plant nutrients such as phosphorus and calcium available, which are often scarce in acidic soils.

- Activation of enzymes: Applying electricity on plants can enable enzymes such as nitrate reductase, which is found in the metabolism of nitrogen. Therefore, plants can easily absorb and use nutrients for better growth and increased yields.

Electromagnetic effects

- Stimulating plant growth: Electroculture can help plants grow by boosting cell division and elongation. This enables booger and stronger plants. Electrical stimulation of plant hormones such as auxins and gibberellins enables cells to divide and grow and is believed to cause this effect.

- Increase in photosynthesis: Electrical stimulation can also boost photosynthesis, which is the process of plants converting energy from light into chemical energy. This enhances plants' growth and increases yields because they have more energy for growth and development.

- Improvement of root development: Electroculture creates larger and more robust root systems for nutrient absorption and plant growth. Electrical stimulation can boost the activity of hormones that help roots grow and develop, such as cytokinins. This can boost root growth and faster development.

Electrophysiological effects

- Increased membrane permeability: Electrical stimulation can make plant cell membranes more permeable for easier absorption of nutrients and water. This can boost plant growth and increase yields, especially in soils with few nutrients.

- Increased uptake of nutrients: Electroculture also helps plants to absorb important nutrients such as nitrogen, phosphorus, and potassium by enabling transport proteins in their roots to work harder.

- Activation of plant growth regulators: Stimulating a plant with electricity can enable plant growth regulators such as abscisic acid and ethylene, which control plants' growth and development. This can boost plant growth and increase yields because these regulators affect various parts of plant growth, such as when seeds sprout, roots grow, and flowers open.

FACTORS AFFECTING THE EFFICIENCY OF ELECTROCULTURE

The following are factors affecting the efficiency of electroculture:

Type of current used

How well electroculture works depends on the type of electrical current used, including AC or DC. Some studies have shown that DC performs well at making plants grow than AC.

Voltage and frequency

The voltage and frequency of the current used in electroculture can also affect its performance. Generally, it has been shown that lower voltages and higher frequencies make plants grow well.

How long it lasts, and when it's used

How well electroculture works can also be affected by how long and when the electrical stimulation is applied. Studies have shown that shorter applications of electrical current more often better enable plants' growth than longer applications.

Electrode material

The type of material used for the electrodes can also change the performance of electroculture. Some studies have shown that electrodes made of noble metals, such as platinum, enable plants to grow more than electrodes made of copper or aluminum.

Types of plants and growth stages

The type of plant and its growth stage can also change the performance of electroculture. Some plants may respond better to electricity than others, and the stage of growth when the electricity is used may also affect its performance.

APPLICATIONS OF ELECTROCULTURE

Crop production

Electroculture could change the way crops are grown by increasing yields and producing healthier and stronger plants. It can also minimize the use of chemical fertilizers and pesticides for a more sustainable and good environment to farm.

Horticulture

Electroculture can also be used in horticulture to enable ornamental plants, such as flowers and shrubs, to grow and get bigger. It can help fruits and vegetables to get better for easier sale.

Forestry

Electroculture can be used in forestry to enable trees to grow and develop in places where the soil lacks enough nutrients or is broken down. It can also make trees more resistant to drought and disease that come from the environment.

Environmental remediation

Electroculture also helps to sanitize the environment by stimulating the growth of plants that can absorb pollutants such as heavy metals and organic compounds and eliminate them through a method known as phytoremediation. This method helps to rebuild ecosystems that have been damaged and enhances the quality of soil and water.

Conclusion

Electroculture works in several ways, such as through chemical, electromagnetic, and electrical effects on the body. These effects can enable plants to grow and increase yields to absorb nutrients, boost photosynthesis, and encourage root growth.

Electroculture could change agriculture and other fields by boosting crop yields, enhancing plant health and vitality, and minimizing the need for chemical fertilizers and pesticides. It also helps to restore ecosystems that have been damaged and to enhance soil and water quality.

Future research on electroculture should prioritize setting standard protocols for using it and testing how well it works with different types of plants and at different stages of growth. We should also explore how electroculture might affect the environment and make safety rules for its use.

In conclusion, electroculture is a great technology that could change agriculture and other fields by enabling plant growth and increasing yields. Its electrochemical, electromagnetic, and electrophysiological effects have helped plants to absorb more nutrients, boost photosynthesis, and support root growth. More research should find the best ways to use it, discover how it might affect the environment, and ensure it can be used safely and effectively.

PART 3: ELECTRODES AND POWER SUPPLIES

TYPES OF ELECTRODES USED IN ELECTROCULTURE

In electroculture, there are different types of electrodes, such as:

1. Copper electrodes

In electroculture, copper electrodes are some of the most frequently used electrodes. They don't cost much and are available. Copper electrodes send electricity to the plant because they conduct electricity well. However, they are prone to rust in alkaline soils. This can release copper ions that plants can't handle.

Advantages

- High electrical conductivity
- It's cheap and easy to get
- Good for sending electricity to the plant

Disadvantages

- Corrosion-prone, especially in alkaline soils
- Copper ions can kill plants if they escape into the air.

2. Zinc electrodes

In electroculture, zinc electrodes are another type of electrode that is frequently used. They aren't too costly, and they also conduct electricity properly. Zinc electrodes are less vulnerable to rust compared to copper electrodes. However, releasing zinc ions can also harm plants.

Advantages

- High electrical conductivity
- They are less likely to rust
- Usually not too costly

Disadvantages

- Zinc ions can kill plants if they escape into the air.

3. Stainless steel electrodes

In electroculture, electrodes made of stainless steel are also frequently used. They are also good at conducting electricity and are less likely to rust. Furthermore, they are strong and durable before replacement. However, they can be more costly than other types of electrodes.

Advantages

- High electrical conductivity
- They are less likely to rust.
- Durable and able to be used for a long time without replacement

Disadvantages

- They are pricey.

4. Graphite electrodes

Another type of electrode used in electroculture is made of graphite. They conduct electricity well and don't react with chemicals, which is ideal in alkaline soils. Graphite electrodes also last a long time and won't rust easily. However, they can be costly compared to other types of electrodes.

Advantages

- Good conductors of electricity
- They don't react with chemicals and are perfect in alkaline soils.
- They are strong and don't rust easily.

Disadvantages

- They are costly.

5. Platinum electrodes

Electrodes made of platinum are the most costly ones used in electroculture. They can't rust and have a high electrical conductivity. Platinum electrodes are perfect in acidic soils, whereas other electrodes might not. However, because of how much they cost, they aren't commonly used in electroculture.

Advantages

- High electrical conductivity
- Resistant to corrosion
- Perfect for acidic soils

Disadvantages

- They are very expensive.

FACTORS INFLUENCING THE CHOICE OF ELECTRODE IN ELECTROCULTURE

In electroculture, the choice of electrode depends on several things, such as:

1. Plant species

Different types of plants have different needs for electroculture. Some plants can handle specific types of electrodes better than others, while others may require a specific type of electrode to grow and develop perfectly.

2. Voltage and current

In electroculture, the choice of electrode is also affected by the voltage and current applied. Some electrodes are fine with high voltage and current, while others may work better with low voltage and current.

3. Duration of electroculture treatment

The length of the electroculture treatment also determines how to choose an electrode. Some electrodes may work best for short-term treatments, while others are better suited to longer-term plans.

In conclusion, Electroculture is an electric farming technique in which low levels of electricity promote plant growth. Electroculture uses electrodes to deliver power directly to the plants and their selection varies based on factors like plant type, voltage/current levels, and duration of treatment; copper, zinc, stainless steel graphite, or platinum electrodes are commonly employed with each having their own set of advantages and disadvantages; more research should be conducted to develop improved electrodes that promote growth while having less of an environmental impact.

POWER SOURCES FOR ELECTROCULTURE

Power sources play a pivotal role in electroculture; without them, applying electric fields to plants and soil would be impossible. In this section, we explore various types of electroculture-oriented power sources as well as what factors need to be taken into consideration when choosing one and their associated advantages/disadvantages.

TYPES OF POWER SOURCES FOR ELECTROCULTURE

Solar Power

Solar power is one of the primary energy sources used in electroculture, consisting of solar panels used to convert sunlight into electricity using photovoltaic cells exposed to sunlight. Not only is solar energy a renewable and clean source of energy but it's also cost-effective since no fuel or maintenance costs need to be covered once panels have been installed.

- Advantages: Washable solar panels provide an environmentally-friendly source of power that's cost-effective over time and require minimal maintenance costs.

- Disadvantages: Weather conditions can alter efficiency, and initial installation costs may be high, these systems do not make economic sense for all businesses.

Wind Power

Electroculture also utilizes wind power as another power source, using wind turbines to convert the kinetic energy of the wind into electricity for generation. Wind energy provides an alternative, renewable, and clean source of energy that can be utilized in both large and small-scale operations; its effectiveness is determined by the available wind.

- Advantages: It provides an eco-friendly, renewable source of energy and can be utilized in both large- and small-scale operations.
- Disadvantages: Wind can affect efficiency; Initial installation costs can be high.

Hydro Power

Hydropower is a reliable and renewable form of energy that is perfect for electroculture applications. Hydropower uses water turbines to create electricity from dams, rivers, or other bodies of water sources and doesn't emit greenhouse gasses into the environment.

- Advantages: Clean energy solution that does not emit greenhouse gas emissions.

- Disadvantages: Whilst solar water heating technology may provide many benefits, its availability may be restricted to areas with sufficient access to freshwater sources and initial installation costs can be considerable.

Geothermal Power

Geothermal power is an eco-friendly source of renewable and reliable energy that Electroculture can utilize. Geothermal energy uses heat from belowground sources to produce electricity without producing greenhouse gas emissions; however, availability may be restricted in regions with geothermal activity.

- Advantages: It offers a renewable and reliable source of energy without producing greenhouse gas emissions

- Disadvantages: Sophisticated control systems may only be suitable in areas with geothermal activity and initial installation costs can be high.

Biomass Power

Biomass power is a renewable source of energy used in electroculture that draws upon organic matter such as wood chips, crop residues, and animal waste to generate electricity. Biomass energy reduces greenhouse gas emissions significantly while also being an eco-friendly option; however, its availability may be limited and production could potentially harm the environment.

- Advantages: Benefits include renewable sources of energy which reduce greenhouse gas emissions; as well as lower operating costs and improve sustainability.

- Disadvantages: For one thing, biomass production could potentially harm the environment and access is sometimes limited.

Fuel Cells

Fuel cells provide an environmentally-friendly and efficient source of energy suitable for Electroculture. Fuel cells generate electricity by converting hydrogen and oxygen into water; without creating greenhouse gas emissions. Their efficiency allows up to 60% of the energy stored within a fuel source to be converted to electricity; however, hydrogen shortages make production costly.

- Advantages: Clean and efficient source of energy that can convert up to 60% of fuel's energy content to electricity.

- Disadvantages: Hydrogen can be scarce and its production is costly.

FACTORS TO CONSIDER IN CHOOSING A POWER SOURCE FOR ELECTROCULTURE

Availability of the Power Source

Considerations should also be given to the accessibility of power sources when selecting an electroculture power source. Some sources such as solar and wind energy may be more accessible in certain regions; you should opt for one which is readily available in your location to ensure an effective operation in terms of reliability and efficiency.

Cost

Affordability is another key consideration when selecting an energy source for Electroculture. The costs include initial installation and equipment expenses as well as ongoing maintenance and operational fees. When making this selection, ensure it fits within your budget constraints.

Efficiency

A reliable power source should also consider its efficiency, which measures the amount of energy it can produce with minimal resources used. A highly efficient source can generate more electricity with reduced fuel or resource consumption - so make sure that your electroculture operation runs as reliably and cost-effectively as possible by selecting such an energy source.

Environmental Impact

A key consideration when selecting your power source should be its environmental impact. Certain options, like biomass power, such as deforestation and soil erosion can harm the environment - therefore you should choose an option with minimal negative repercussions that support sustainable farming practices.

Reliability

A reliable power source is an integral element to consider for any successful electroculture operation. Choose one with backup power to prevent power outages.

Conclusion

Electroculture's best power source will depend upon your specific circumstances and goals when choosing one, from reliable operations with cost-effectiveness to environmental sustainability. Considerations when selecting your power source should include availability, cost, efficiency, environmental impact, and reliability as factors when making this selection decision. Each power source offers advantages and disadvantages; select one which meets all these criteria best.

METHODS FOR MEASURING ELECTRICAL CURRENT AND VOLTAGE

Electrical current and voltage are important concepts in electrical engineering and physics. Electrical current is defined as the flow of electric charge through a conductor, typically measured in amperes (A). Current flows from positive to negative polarity - contrary to electron movement. Voltage, on the other hand, measures potential differences between two points within an electric circuit, usually measured in volts (V). Voltage acts like an impulse driving the flow of electrons along conductors.

Measuring electrical current and voltage is crucial for several reasons, including:

- Ensuring safe operation: Measuring current and voltage can ensure safe operation for electrical devices and systems, particularly high voltage applications where an unexpected spike could damage equipment or pose a safety threat to personnel. This process is especially important in high-voltage settings where an unexpected voltage or current spike could prove damaging or hazardous to workers' health and safety.

- Troubleshooting electrical problems: Measuring electrical current and voltage helps identify the cause of electrical problems. For instance, if a device is acting oddly, measuring current and voltage measurements will provide insight into whether it stems from faulty components or wiring issues.

- Maintaining optimal performance: Measuring electrical current and voltage can ensure devices are operating at optimal performance levels. For instance, measuring an electric motor's voltage and current can ensure it operates at the appropriate speed and torque levels.

- Design and Development: Measuring electrical current and voltage is integral to the design and development of electronic devices and systems. By taking measurements from prototype devices, engineers can identify potential design flaws early and make necessary corrections.

In conclusion, measuring electrical current and voltage is essential in ensuring the safe and optimal operation of electrical devices and systems, troubleshooting electrical issues, and supporting new technological development.

ELECTRICAL CURRENT MEASUREMENT METHODS

There are various methods available to you for measuring electrical current. Here are three popular ones:

- Ammeter: An ammeter is an instrument for measuring electric current in a circuit. It typically connects in series with it and allows its flow through it; ammeters come in both analog and digital forms with various sensitivities and accuracies to measure flow rates from low-voltage power transmission lines up to small electronic devices that draw current through it.

- Clamp Meter: Also referred to as a current clamp or probe, clamp meters are ammeters designed to measure current without disrupting its flow in any way. The clamp meter has a hinged jaw that can be opened and clamped around the conductor carrying the current. An electrical signal proportional to the current is created by the clamp meter, which converts the magnetic field generated in it by the current flowing through the conductor. Clamp meters are often used in applications where it is impossible to break the circuit, such as measuring the current draw of appliances or monitoring the current flow in electrical panels.

- Hall Effect Sensor: A Hall effect sensor is a solid-state device used for measuring magnetic fields. When applied perpendicularly to one, its output voltage reflects its strength; using this technique to measure current through conductors by placing one near them and measuring their magnetic fields creates. As its method does not involve breaking circuits or cutting wires, safety considerations do not arise as often.

Each method offers its advantages and disadvantages; therefore, selecting the optimal approach depends on each specific application as well as desired levels of accuracy and convenience.

ELECTRICAL VOLTAGE MEASUREMENT METHODS

There are multiple methods available for measuring electrical voltage, each offering its own set of advantages and disadvantages. Here are three of them:

- Voltmeter: Voltmeters are instruments designed to measure the potential difference between two points in an electrical circuit. Both analog and digital models exist, offering various sensitivities and accuracy levels when measuring voltage differences between circuit points. Voltmeters have multiple applications such as monitoring battery voltage levels or tracking output from power supplies.

- Oscilloscope: An oscilloscope is a device used to display and analyze electrical signal waves. This includes measuring the voltage of AC or DC signals as well as their frequency, phase, and other characteristics of them. Oscilloscopes come in both analog and digital formats with various sensitivities and accuracy levels that may be employed during electronic design or troubleshooting processes.

- Multimeter: A multimeter is an instrument capable of accurately gauging voltage, current, and resistance measurements. Available in both analog and digital forms with various sensitivities and accuracy capabilities to suit varying uses from measuring battery voltage to troubleshooting issues in appliances or electronic devices.

Each method offers its own set of advantages and disadvantages; choosing one ultimately depends on your particular application as well as desired accuracy and convenience levels. A voltmeter is typically the best tool for measuring voltage in circuits; an oscilloscope excels at analyzing waveforms; finally, a multimeter is a versatile instrument capable of measuring voltage, current, and resistance as well.

COMPARATIVE METHODS

There are various techniques for measuring electrical current and voltage available today, each offering unique advantages and disadvantages. Here is a comparison between the three of them on various criteria:

- Accuracy: Accuracy in measurements refers to how closely measured values correspond with actual ones. All three methods typically produce accurate readings within their specified ranges. Clamp meters may suffer due to orientation issues and the presence of nearby conductors affecting their accuracy.

- Precision: Precision of measurements measures how consistent measurements are when repeated multiple times. Digital instruments like multimeters and oscilloscopes generally tend to provide greater precision than analog instruments like ammeters and voltmeters.

- Range: The range of measurements refers to the maximum and minimum values that an instrument is capable of measuring. Ammeters and voltmeters generally have fixed range capabilities, while clamp meters, oscilloscopes, and multimeters often boast wider-ranging measurement capacities.

- Cost: When selecting instruments for both hobbyists and small businesses, cost should always be an important factor. Analog instruments usually tend to be less costly than digital ones; however, this could differ based on the brand and features of each instrument.

- Ease of Use: The ease of using any instrument depends on its complexity, the level of experience of its user, and its specific application. In general, clamp meters and digital multimeters tend to be easier for novice users, while oscilloscopes often require greater expertise to operate effectively.

As previously discussed, selecting an electrical current and voltage measuring method depends upon the specifics of your application and desired level of accuracy, precision, range, cost, and ease of use. Ammeters and voltmeters tend to be straightforward solutions, while clamp meters, oscilloscopes, and multimeters offer greater versatility.

Conclusion

Measurement of electric current and voltage are integral components of many applications, from electronic design to power system analysis. There are various methods available for measuring electrical current and voltage; each has its own set of advantages and disadvantages.

Ammeters are among the most frequently utilized instruments for electrical current measurement. Their straightforward design makes them simple to use and provides accurate results within their range. Clamp meters and Hall effect sensors may offer other advantages that include non-contact measurements as well as low current measurements.

Voltmeters are among the most frequently utilized instruments for electrical voltage measurement, providing easy and accurate readings within their range. Other measurement instruments, including oscilloscopes and multimeters, offer more flexible solutions enabling users to analyze waveforms as well as measure current and resistance alongside voltage measurements.

When selecting a measurement method, several key considerations must be kept in mind, including accuracy, precision, range, cost, and ease of use. Your application and desired level of measurement capabilities also factor into this decision.

Users who know about various methods for measuring electrical current and voltage, along with factors that should be taken into consideration when selecting their method of choice, can make informed decisions that ensure accurate, reliable measurements in their work.

PART 4: APPLICATIONS OF ELECTROCULTURE

ELECTROCULTURE IN AGRICULTURE

Agriculture refers to the practice of cultivating land, growing crops, and raising animals to harvest food or fiber products from them for commercial sale or consumption. Agriculture practices involve various tasks like soil preparation, planting, harvesting, and animal husbandry as part of this production chain. Agriculture has always played an integral part in human civilization as an essential means for providing food security, maintaining communities, and stimulating economic development - its innovations make modern agriculture increasingly efficient, productive, and environmentally friendly.

Electroculture has emerged as an alternative approach to traditional agricultural practices, providing an eco-friendly solution to address environmental and economic challenges facing agriculture. Agriculture accounts for nearly one-third of global greenhouse gas emissions; using electroculture can offer a sustainable and eco-friendly way of mitigating its negative effects on the environment.

Electroculture's greatest advantage lies in its potential to boost crop yields. By applying low voltage electrical charges directly to soil or plants, electroculture can stimulate plant growth and boost nutrient uptake resulting in healthier plants that produce larger harvests - thus improving yields overall. Furthermore, electroculture helps crops adapt better to environmental stressors like drought, heat, or cold, which may impact them significantly and reduce yield loss.

Electroculture can help enhance soil quality by increasing microbial activity in the soil, which is necessary for cycling nutrients and decomposing organic matter. Promoting beneficial microorganism growth through electroculture helps keep the soil healthy while decreasing synthetic fertilizer requirements and runoff risks - both essential aspects to protecting nearby water sources from degradation.

Electroculture's most prominent use in agriculture is water conservation. Accessing freshwater resources is often scarce in many regions around the world, particularly arid and semi-arid regions, so electroculture offers another effective tool for water conservation by encouraging more efficient plant water usage by improving root systems and nutrient uptake, thus decreasing the need for irrigation.

Electroculture offers another key application in agriculture for pest and disease management: by stimulating plant growth and improving immunity systems, electroculture can make plants more resistant to pests and diseases and less reliant on synthetic pesticides, which are harmful both environmentally and can have negative health repercussions.

Overall, electroculture can revolutionize agriculture by providing a sustainable and eco-friendly solution for crop production. By decreasing dependence on synthetic inputs, while encouraging plant health improvement, electroculture can significantly improve yields while simultaneously decreasing the environmental impact associated with agriculture.

Electroculture is an emerging technology with immense potential to transform agriculture. Its benefits include higher crop yields, enhanced soil quality, and water conservation benefits, as well as decreased synthetic input usage. More research needs to be conducted into its mechanisms as well as any limitations or risks; nevertheless, electroculture offers significant potential to meet rising food demands in an eco-friendly fashion.

APPLICATIONS OF ELECTROCULTURE IN AGRICULTURE

Increased Crop Yield:

ElectroCulture has been found to have a considerable impact on crop yield, with some studies reporting yield increases of up to 30%. Electric current stimulates plant growth while simultaneously improving the absorption of nutrients and water from the soil, leading to larger and healthier plants overall.

ElectroCulture can boost nutrient uptake by neutralizing any electrical charges between plant roots and soil. Such charges may impede nutrients from entering into their roots; by applying a small electric current to neutralize these charges, more nutrients can be freely absorbed by your roots.

ElectroCulture can also help improve a plant's ability to absorb water from its soil environment. By breaking apart soil particles and making water penetrate more deeply into the ground, ElectroCulture reduces how much is lost through evaporation while making it more available to plant roots.

ElectroCulture can not only enhance nutrient and water uptake but can also increase photosynthesis - the process by which plants convert light to energy - by stimulating plant chloroplasts responsible for photosynthesis. By doing this, ElectroCulture helps boost overall plant energy production leading to larger and healthier plants.

Improved Soil Quality:

ElectroCulture can have an amazing impact on soil quality. Electric current stimulation stimulates microbial activity in the soil, leading to faster breakdown of organic matter and making more nutrients accessible to plants - creating an ideal environment for their growth.

Microorganisms play an essential part in soil health, breaking down organic material and recycling nutrients. ElectroCulture can stimulate this essential function to create more conducive conditions for plant growth by encouraging microbial activity within soil structures and fertility.

ElectroCulture can also assist in reducing soil compaction, an increasingly widespread issue across agricultural systems. Soil compaction occurs when soil particles become tightly packed together, making it hard for air and water to pass freely through it - leading to reduced crop yields and soil degradation. By employing small electric currents, ElectroCulture helps break apart these particles making for more porous soil that reduces compaction.

Water Conservation:

ElectroCulture can assist farmers with water conservation by breaking up soil particles to allow more moisture into the ground, decreasing evaporation losses while still meeting crop yield targets. Farmers can thus use less water while still reaping similar harvest yields.

ElectroCulture can not only help reduce water loss but can also enhance irrigation system efficiency by making more water available to plant roots and decreasing how much is required for irrigation, helping save both time and money on irrigation costs. This way, farmers can make greater water savings without incurring higher expenses on their bills for services rendered.

Pest and disease management:

ElectroCulture can also help manage pests and diseases in crops by stimulating natural defense mechanisms within plants to ward off pests and diseases on their own. By stimulating plant defense systems with electrical current, ElectroCulture may reduce the need for chemical pesticides and herbicides as the plant becomes better equipped to defend itself against such attacks on its own.

ElectroCulture can boost a plant's natural defenses in multiple ways, one being by increasing the production of phytochemicals - compounds produced by plants to protect themselves against pests and diseases. By stimulating production with electrical current, farmers can stimulate this production, making plants more resistant to pests and diseases.

ElectroCulture can also help minimize the effect of soil-borne diseases, which are difficult to manage using traditional means. By stimulating microbial activity in the soil, ElectroCulture creates an environment less conducive for disease-causing pathogens to thrive - leading to less incidence and severity of soil-borne illnesses and healthier crops as a result.

ElectroCulture could transform agriculture, by increasing crop yields, improving soil quality, conserving water use, and decreasing chemical pesticide and herbicide usage. Farmers using small electric currents can stimulate plant growth while improving nutrient and water uptake as well as supporting soil health through ElectroCulture technology. Its environmental benefits also make its potential apparent; using it may reduce both water usage and chemical inputs for agriculture, reducing overall impact and decreasing environmental footprints associated with farming practices. Although much remains to be discovered regarding its full capabilities it's clear this technology could revolutionize how food is produced today.

ADVANTAGES OF ELECTROCULTURE IN AGRICULTURE

Reduce reliance on synthetic inputs:

ElectroCulture can significantly decrease dependence on synthetic inputs such as chemical fertilizers and pesticides, which can be costly and cause environmental issues like soil degradation, water pollution, and biodiversity loss. By using ElectroCulture to increase plant growth and nutrient uptake rates more effectively, farmers can decrease dependence on such inputs resulting in a more sustainable and eco-friendly agricultural system.

Eco-Friendly:

ElectroCulture offers multiple eco-friendly advantages. No harmful chemicals or genetically modified organisms (GMOs) are necessary, making it a safer and more sustainable farming alternative to conventional farming techniques. Furthermore, by decreasing synthetic input usage ElectroCulture helps lower greenhouse gas emissions and water pollution impact from agriculture.

Low Cost:

ElectroCulture is a cost-effective technology designed for use by farmers themselves, requiring no special training or expensive equipment - instead using just copper wire, batteries, and electrodes - making it particularly suitable for smaller-scale farmers without access to large capital investments.

ElectroCulture can also assist farmers in cutting costs by increasing crop yields and decreasing synthetic input usage - leading to more profits in areas with limited resources.

ElectroCulture can offer numerous advantages to both farmers and the environment. By decreasing synthetic input use, ElectroCulture helps create a more sustainable and eco-friendly agricultural system. Furthermore, as it's a low-cost technology easily implemented by farmers themselves, ElectroCulture makes an appealing solution for small-scale operations. As ElectroCulture advances further it has the potential to transform food production practices - creating more eco-friendly agriculture practices while also increasing yield efficiency.

LIMITATIONS OF ELECTROCULTURE IN AGRICULTURE

Limited research and knowledge:

ElectroCulture is an emerging field of agriculture that utilizes low-voltage electric charges to enhance plant growth and soil health, in a sustainable and eco-friendly manner. While ElectroCulture has gained prominence as a viable farming solution, more research needs to be conducted regarding its long-term effects on plant growth, soil health, and the environment.

One of the primary drawbacks to ElectroCulture is a lack of research conducted in its field. While studies on using electrical charges to enhance plant growth and soil health often focus on short-term effects, little is understood regarding long-term stimulation by electrical charges on plant growth or health; as a result, optimal voltage, frequency, duration of electrical charges have yet to be fully established; making standardized protocols difficult.

ElectroCulture may have an environmental impact that needs to be examined closely; while considered a sustainable and eco-friendly farming method, its environmental ramifications require further examination - especially since its usage includes electricity which could have potentially negative side effects if mismanaged. This research should take place as soon as possible as well.

As more research and knowledge regarding ElectroCulture are still scarce, additional fieldwork must be conducted in this field. Such studies should examine the long-term impacts of electrical charges on plant growth, soil health, and the environment; their optimal parameters for stimulation; as well as any possible impacts this form of agriculture could have on soil microorganisms, plant growth, or crop yield.

Potential adverse impact on soil microorganisms:

Soil microorganisms play an essential role in maintaining soil health and fertility by decomposing organic matter and cycling nutrients through their systems, and contributing to the formation of soil structure while suppressing plant pathogens. Unfortunately, ElectroCulture may have negative impacts on these important ecosystem components.

Electrical charges on soil microorganisms may lead to changes in their diversity. Soil communities are sensitive to environmental changes, and exposure to electrical charges could reduce microbial diversity resulting in adverse consequences on both health and fertility, with reduced nutrient cycling and structure formation occurring as a result.

Electric charges could also hurt soil microorganisms by changing their nutrient availability. Soil microorganisms play an essential role in cycling nutrients back into the soil, and their activity is essential to their availability; however, exposure to electrical charges could disrupt this vital cycle, altering soil microbial activity and leading to changes in nutrient availability that affect plant growth and yield.

Finally, electrical charges could disrupt the delicate balance between soil microbial communities and plant pathogens, potentially leading to their proliferation. Soil microbiology plays an integral part in suppressing plant pathogens; any disruption could have devastating repercussions for crop yield.

To mitigate any negative impacts of ElectroCulture on soil microorganisms, care must be taken when applying electrical charges. This involves evaluating optimal parameters for electrical stimulation as well as using inoculants that promote microbial activity and maintain diversity; alternatively, organic farming practices which promote health and fertility may help limit potential negative repercussions from ElectroCulture on microorganisms.

Conclusion

ElectroCulture is an emerging agricultural field that utilizes low voltage electrical charges to accelerate plant growth and soil health, as well as increase crop yield, water conservation efforts, pest and disease management, as well as conservation. ElectroCulture works by creating a flow of ions that stimulate plant growth and nutrient absorption resulting in higher crop yield, improved soil quality, and pest and disease management.

ElectroCulture farming methods offer numerous advantages over traditional farming techniques, including reduced synthetic input use, eco-friendliness, and lower costs. Unfortunately, it also comes with certain drawbacks like limited research knowledge and potential negative consequences to soil microorganisms.

To fully realize the advantages of ElectroCulture, additional research should be undertaken on its long-term effects on plant growth, soil health, and the environment. This should include evaluating optimal parameters for electrical stimulation as well as the potential impacts of ElectroCulture on soil microorganisms, plant growth, and crop yield. Likewise, standardized protocols for ElectroCulture should be established to promote widespread adoption.

ElectroCulture holds immense potential as a sustainable and eco-friendly farming method and must be investigated to fully comprehend its full scope of adoption in agriculture. However, its limitations must also be fully investigated to fully grasp its full potential for widespread adoption in farming practices.

ELECTROCULTURE IN HORTICULTURE

Horticulture is the science, art, and practice of cultivating plants - particularly fruits, vegetables, flowers, and ornamental plants - for human use and pleasure. This practice encompasses propagation, cultivation, fertilization, irrigation, pest management, and harvesting - with skilled horticulturists using knowledge in botany, plant physiology, soil science, and environmental science to produce attractive, nutritious plants that add value to our surroundings. Horticulture plays an integral part in food security, environmental sustainability, and aesthetic enhancement.

One of the main benefits of ElectroCulture in horticulture is promoting plant growth and development. Low-voltage electrical charges create a flow of ions that stimulate plant metabolism, leading to faster growth, improved development, and higher crop yield and quality. Furthermore, ElectroCulture has also been proven to improve uniformity and consistency among crops resulting in superior produce - ideal for horticulturists looking to promote high-value fruits and vegetables that increase market value.

ElectroCulture can significantly enhance plant nutrition by improving their uptake of nutrients from soil or hydroponic solutions, making absorption simpler for plants to access nutrient sources like soil or hydroponic solutions for better plant nutrition. This is particularly useful for hydroponic practices where plant roots rely heavily on these nutrient solutions for growth. ElectroCulture also prevents leaching to ensure optimal nutrient availability to plants.

ElectroCulture can also be utilized for pest and disease management in horticulture. ElectroCulture's electrical charge can kill or repel pests such as mites, aphids, and thrips without resorting to synthetic pesticides; thus lowering environmental impacts associated with farming practices like horticulture. Furthermore, ElectroCulture enhances plants' natural defense mechanisms against pests and diseases for healthier plants with increased resistance to common diseases.

ElectroCulture can also improve soil quality. ElectroCulture's electrical charge breaks apart soil particles to make more nutrients available to plants, leading to better structure, water retention, and aeration in turn resulting in greater soil fertility and overall health benefits, making ElectroCulture ideal for nursery or greenhouse practices alike. Furthermore, ElectroCulture encourages beneficial soil microorganisms like mycorrhizal fungi which aid in nutrient uptake as well as plant growth.

ElectroCulture farming is an eco-friendly method that reduces synthetic inputs to ensure greater sustainability, thus lessening its environmental impact and providing small farmers with increased economic opportunities. Furthermore, its low costs make ElectroCulture accessible for small-scale farming operations and make its application accessible to large-scale operations as a result of being easily accessible for larger-scale farmers.

ElectroCulture holds great potential benefits for horticulture, yet also poses some limitations. Unfortunately, research and knowledge regarding its long-term impacts are currently limited - in particular concerning plant growth, soil health, and environmental effects. Thus more investigation must be done on optimal parameters for electrical stimulation as well as its potential effect on soil microorganisms, plant growth, and crop yield.

ElectroCulture is an important innovation in horticulture that could transform farming practices. It improves plant growth and development, soil quality, and synthetic input usage while being eco-friendly, potentially opening up economic opportunities, increasing food security, and decreasing environmental impact. Further research is required to understand its long-term effects as well as develop standard protocols for its implementation in agriculture.

APPLICATIONS OF ELECTROCULTURE IN HORTICULTURE

ElectroCulture can be applied in numerous horticulture applications, providing an innovative and effective form of farming. Here we explore its many uses within horticulture.

- Fruits and Vegetables: Electroculture can help increase the growth, yield, and quality of fruits and vegetables. Electrical current stimulates plant cells that facilitate photosynthesis, nutrient uptake, root development, and root system health resulting in faster growth, larger fruit/veggies with higher nutritional content as well as delaying their ripening process for extended shelf life.

- Ornamental Plants: Electroculture can also be utilized in the cultivation of ornamental plants such as flowers and foliage plants. An electric current can stimulate plant growth while simultaneously improving the color, fragrance, shape, size, and shape of flowers or foliage plants resulting in more vibrant and attractive ornamental specimens.

- Hydroponics: Electroculture can be applied in hydroponic systems, which are soilless methods of growing plants, to promote faster growth and higher yields. Electrical current can stimulate plant roots to absorb nutrients more readily for faster development and faster yields. Electroculture may also help prevent or treat diseases in hydroponic environments.

Electroculture holds immense potential to transform how we cultivate plants in horticulture. By harnessing electric currents to promote plant growth and development, electroculture could revolutionize this field - increasing yields while improving quality while decreasing pesticide and fertilizer usage. More research needs to be conducted to fully comprehend its long-term sustainability effects on the growth and development processes of plants.

ADVANTAGES OF ELECTROCULTURE IN HORTICULTURE

ElectroCulture in Horticulture provides numerous advantages over traditional farming methods. Here we discuss these advantages of ElectroCulture for Horticulture.

- Eco-friendliness: ElectroCulture is an eco-friendly farming method, as it does not rely on synthetic inputs like fertilizers and pesticides, minimizing its environmental impact while making it a sustainable farming technique. Furthermore, ElectroCulture reduces carbon emissions by eliminating synthetic fertilizers while cutting fossil fuel consumption in equipment operations.

- Reduced Reliance on Synthetic Inputs: ElectroCulture significantly decreases its use of synthetic inputs such as fertilizers, pesticides, and herbicides compared with traditional gardening, thus decreasing both environmental impact and costs associated with these inputs. Furthermore, ElectroCulture enhances the natural defense mechanisms of plants, further decreasing the need for synthetic pesticides and herbicides.

- Low Cost: ElectroCulture is an economical method of farming that requires minimal inputs and equipment, producing electricity using a low-voltage source for inexpensive cultivation. ElectroCulture can increase crop yields while improving quality to provide higher profits to farmers.

- Water Conservation: ElectroCulture promotes water conservation through improved soil structure and retention. An electrical charge breaks apart soil particles to increase porosity for better absorption and retention, which reduces water usage for horticulture while making this farming method more sustainable.

ElectroCulture offers many advantages over traditional farming methods in horticulture. As an eco-friendly, low-cost, and sustainable method, ElectroCulture reduces synthetic input reliance and promotes water conservation; all of which lead to improved economic opportunities, improved food security, and reduced environmental impact. ElectroCulture should therefore be seriously considered as a viable solution in horticulture.

LIMITATIONS OF ELECTROCULTURE IN HORTICULTURE

ElectroCulture can bring many advantages over traditional farming methods; however, there are also certain limitations of ElectroCulture when used for horticulture. Here we discuss those limitations of ElectroCulture.

- Limited Research and Knowledge: ElectroCulture has been used for several decades now, yet little research and understanding exists on its effectiveness and possible impacts. More studies are necessary to ascertain the optimal voltage and frequency levels for specific crops and soil types as well as understand their long-term effects on both soil quality and plant growth.

- Potential Negative Impact on Soil Microorganisms: ElectroCulture could potentially have negative repercussions for soil microorganisms. An electrical charge could alter microbial populations in the soil and disrupt ecosystem processes affecting nutrient cycling and ecosystem functioning; more research must be completed to ascertain its full scope and how best it may be mitigated.

- Safety risks: ElectroCulture involves the use of electricity, which poses potential safety risks if handled incorrectly. Farmers and workers must receive proper training in the safe operation of electrical equipment to prevent accidents from happening.

ElectroCulture can offer many advantages for horticulture, yet certain limitations must be considered when using ElectroCulture as an agricultural method. Limited research on its effectiveness and potential impacts, potential negative impact on soil microorganisms, and potential safety hazards should all be taken into consideration and addressed appropriately in terms of further research or proper handling of electrical equipment. By addressing these restrictions ElectroCulture may remain an attractive and sustainable method for agricultural endeavors.

FUTURE RESEARCH AND POTENTIAL FOR WIDESPREAD ADOPTION

Electroculture is an emerging horticultural technology with great potential to revolutionize how plants are grown. Although much remains to learn about electroculture, here are some areas for future research and possible adoption:

- Long-Term Impact of ElectroCulture on Plant Growth, Yield, and Quality: Further research needs to be conducted into the long-term effects of electroculture on plant growth, yield, and quality. While short-term studies have produced promising results from electroculture treatments, further examination of its impact over multiple growing seasons is key in understanding its long-term effectiveness as well as any possible negative repercussions associated with its use.

- Impact of ElectroCulture on Soil Health and Microbial Communities: Electroculture could affect soil health and microbial communities, including its beneficial and harmful microbe balance in the soil. More research needs to be done into its impact and how best it can be integrated with other practices for improving soil health.

- Optimizing ElectroCulture for Maximum Benefits: More research must be conducted to maximize electroculture's benefits, including identifying the most efficient electrical frequencies and intensities for different plant species, stages of development, environmental conditions, and placement options of electrodes - these studies should also identify where best they should be placed to make use of electrical energy efficiently.

- Electroculture offers many potential advantages, but overcoming any potential barriers to adoption may prove more challenging than anticipated. Such barriers include cost and energy issues, limited knowledge about its applications, or regulatory obstacles. To overcome such hurdles, education and outreach efforts may need to be put forth to increase awareness and understanding about electroculture as well as research that produces more affordable yet efficient systems and devices for electroculture use.

Conclusion

Electroculture is an emerging technology in horticulture that could dramatically change how we grow plants. By harnessing electrical currents to stimulate plant growth and development, electroculture may enhance plant yields while decreasing pesticide and fertilizer use.

Electroculture can accelerate growth, enhance nutrient uptake and extend the shelf life of fruits and vegetables; ornamental plants benefit from enhanced color, fragrance, and shape to produce more vibrant plants; while hydroponic systems use electroculture to accelerate nutrient uptake while treating or preventing diseases.

Further research must be completed to understand the effects of electroculture on plant growth and development, soil health, and microbial communities. Furthermore, electroculture may face barriers such as its cost or energy use, or lack of knowledge of its technology preventing widespread adoption.

Therefore, further research and adoption of electroculture are warranted in the horticulture industry. With increased development efforts, electroculture can potentially become a more sustainable and efficient method for cultivating plants resulting in agriculture that can better preserve resources over time.

ELECTROCULTURE IN VITICULTURE

Viticulture is the science and practice of cultivating grapes specifically for wine production, using methods such as planting and pruning grapevines until harvesting and processing are complete. Viticulturists utilize their knowledge of plant physiology, soil science, climate regulation, pest management, and preservation of heritage varieties to ensure the optimal growth and quality of grapes produced for winemaking. Viticulture forms an essential component of the global wine industry which holds economic, cultural, and social value worldwide.

Electroculture has long been used in viticulture to improve grape quality and increase the growth and yield of grapevines. Electrodes placed close to the roots of grapevines create an electrical field that stimulates plant growth while strengthening resistance to environmental stresses like drought, frost, or disease.

ADVANTAGES OF ELECTROCULTURE IN VITICULTURE

Electroculture offers several advantages when applied to viticulture. These benefits include:

- Improved Plant Growth: Electrodes placed in the soil generate an electrical field that stimulates plant growth and development, leading to greater yield and quality from grape harvests.

- Resistance To Pest and Diseases: Electroculture has been proven to strengthen plants' resistance against diseases and pests, thus decreasing the need for pesticides or other chemical treatments.

- Increase Drought Tolerance: Electroculture has been proven to increase drought tolerance in plants, lowering their risk of crop failure during dry periods and helping them survive longer.

- Enhance nutrient uptake: The electrical field generated by electrodes stimulates grapevine roots to increase their ability to take in more nutrients from the soil.

CHALLENGES AND LIMITATIONS OF ELECTROCULTURE IN VITICULTURE

Equipment and maintenance expenses associated with electroculture:

One of the main difficulties of electroculture for vineyards is the high cost and maintenance required of its equipment, particularly electrodes. While purchasing expensive equipment may help ensure the proper operation of the system, regular checks to maintain it could become prohibitively expensive, making adoption even harder for smaller vineyards.

Lack of insight into the long-term impacts of electroculture:

Electroculture presents another challenge to viticulture due to our limited understanding of its long-term impacts on grapevines and soil health. While studies have demonstrated positive outcomes on plant growth and yield, we still do not fully comprehend how electroculture may influence a vine's overall health or longevity in terms of longevity and overall well-being - further research needs to take place before conclusively understanding any long-term ramifications of electroculture use in grape growing.

Possible adverse consequences on soil health and microbial communities:

Electroculture may have adverse repercussions for soil health and microbiological communities, with electrodes potentially disrupting the natural balance of microbes in the soil, leading to decreased fertility and overall plant health.

Regulation Hurdles:

Furthermore, regulatory hurdles can impede the use of electroculture in viticulture. Regulations around electrical equipment use and their impact on the environment can differ between regions, making it harder for vineyards to implement this technology. Likewise, no clear guidelines exist regarding its safe usage in vineyards.

KEY CONSIDERATIONS FOR ELECTROCULTURE IN VITICULTURE

Electroculture for viticulture must consider several key factors, including:

- Optimal Electrical Frequency and Intensity: Depending on the grape variety and growing conditions, electroculture requires selecting an optimal frequency and intensity combination to avoid overstimulation of plants or damage to roots. Appropriate steps must be taken so as not to overstimulate or harm roots.

- Electrode Placement: Electrode placement is critical to successful electroculture. Electrodes should be placed near the roots of grapevines, and their position should be altered as their vines grow.

- Timing and Duration of Electroculture Treatment: The timing and duration of electroculture treatments will depend upon the specific grape variety and growing conditions, so treatments must be applied at an ideal time and duration to avoid overstimulating plants or damaging roots.

- Safety Considerations: Since electroculture involves electrical equipment, safety should always be prioritized. To remain compliant with safety guidelines and ensure the equipment is maintained and operated by trained personnel.

FUTURE RESEARCH DIRECTIONS IN ELECTROCULTURE VITICULTURE

Investigation into optimal electroculture treatment conditions:

Optimal electroculture treatment conditions refer to the investigation of optimal conditions under which electroculture can be applied to grapevines to maximize its benefits, which includes exploring various parameters involved in electroculture such as duration, frequency, intensity, and polarity of an applied electric field. By identifying optimal electroculture treatment conditions grape growers can maximize yield, quality, and disease resistance benefits of electroculture application.

Determination of electroculture effects on grape flavor and aroma:

Electroculture has been demonstrated to significantly affect the composition of grape juice and wine, including changes to acidity levels, sugar concentration levels, and phenolic compounds. Therefore, studies must be done on how electroculture impacts the flavor and aroma of grapes as well as the wine produced from them; understanding its impact can assist wine growers and winemakers in producing higher-quality wine products that satisfy consumer tastes.

Study of the long-term impact of electroculture on grapevine health and productivity:

Long-term studies are critical to accurately evaluate the effect of electroculture on grapevine health and productivity, such as monitoring growth, yield, fruit quality, and fruit longevity over several years to ascertain the long-term effects of electroculture as a viticulture practice. Such analyses help establish its sustainability while simultaneously decreasing chemical inputs into vineyards.

Assessment of electroculture for grapevine cultivars:

Different cultivars of grapevine have distinct traits, making it essential to evaluate electroculture's effectiveness for each cultivar. To do this, it is necessary to study each grapevine's response to electroculture including its growth, yield, and fruit quality - this allows grape growers to identify which cultivars are the best candidates for electroculture and which ones should not. By selecting suitable cultivars for electroculture they can improve vineyard management practices while simultaneously increasing profitability.

Conclusion

Electroculture represents an effective strategy to enhance viticultural practices by improving plant growth, yield, and fruit quality while decreasing pesticide and fertilizer usage. Electroculture equipment and maintenance costs, lack of knowledge regarding its long-term effects on soil health and microorganism communities, as well as regulatory hurdles present significant obstacles and limitations to the widespread adoption of electroculture technologies. To overcome these hurdles, more research must be conducted to establish optimal electroculture treatment conditions and assess its effects on grape flavor, aroma, health, and productivity of vines as well as various cultivars of grapevines. Electroculture holds great promise as an innovation that could dramatically change viticultural practices and provide sustainable solutions to the grape and wine industries. Therefore, encouraging further research and adoption of electroculture in viticulture to reach its full potential in the future is imperative to unlock its full potential.

ELECTROCULTURE IN AQUAPONICS AND HYDROPONICS
OVERVIEW OF ELECTROCULTURE APPLICATION IN AQUAPONICS

Aquaponics is a sustainable farming system that combines aquaculture (the raising of aquatic animals such as fish) with hydroponics (plant cultivation in water). Aquaponic systems combine fish and plants for sustainable agriculture in an interdependent relationship, with fish waste providing essential nutrients for plant growth, while plants filter water purifying it for the fish. Aquaponics systems operate in a closed-loop cycle whereby water is recycled for reuse, thus minimizing usage and waste. Aquaponics has become an efficient and sustainable farming method that produces vegetables, herbs, fruit, tilapia trout, or catfish species with little environmental impact.

Electroculture in aquaponics involves passing a small electrical current through the water in an aquaponics system to encourage plant growth and enhance overall plant health. Electrodes placed within the system allow users to control both its intensity and frequency to achieve optimal results.

Advantages Of Electroculture In Aquaponics

- Increased Plant Growth: Electroculture can boost plant growth in aquaponics systems, leading to larger and healthier plants.

- Improved Nutrient Uptake: Electrical current can assist plants in better-absorbing nutrients, benefitting their overall health and ensuring optimal growth.

- Increased Fish Health: Electroculture can also have a beneficial impact on fish health, as its increased plant growth helps improve water quality in your system.

- Reduced Need For Fertilizers: By improving nutrient uptake and plant growth, electroculture can significantly lower fertilizer needs in an aquaponics system.

Challenges And Limitations Of ElectroCulture In Aquaponics

- High Cost of Electroculture Equipment and Maintenance: For many aquaponics growers, electroculture equipment costs can be an obstacle to their business. Initial investment may be significant while ongoing maintenance fees could also pose a problem.

- Needs For Further Investigation of Its Long-term Effects: While electroculture has shown promise in short-term studies, little research exists on its long-term impacts in aquaponics systems. Potential ramifications on plant and fish health, water quality, and overall system productivity must be understood better before electroculture can become widely adopted.

- Potential Negative Impact on Fish Health and Productivity: Electroculture in aquaponics has the potential to have detrimental impacts on both fish health and productivity, such as excessive electrical current harming them and disrupting their behavior, ultimately harming both overall system health and productivity.

- Regulatory Hurdles: Electroculture may face some regulatory hurdles and approval processes in aquaponics systems if it involves using electrical equipment not currently approved for aquaculture or agriculture use. Growers may need to navigate regulatory requirements and obtain permits before beginning this type of cultivation in their systems.

Key Considerations For Electroculture In Aquaponics

- Optimal Electrical Frequency And Intensity: For optimal results, both its frequency and intensity must be carefully managed to achieve optimal results. Too much electricity could harm plants and fish while too little may not have any noticeable impact.

- Electrode Placement: Care should be taken when placing electrodes in an aquaponics system to ensure an evenly distributed current that does not harm fish.

- Timing and Duration of Electoculture Treatment: Electroculture treatments must be carefully planned to minimize overexposure to electric current, which may damage plants or fish.

- Safety Considerations: Safety should always be the top priority when employing electroculture in aquaponics. All electrical components should be properly installed and grounded before beginning any treatments with electroculture, while any potential hazards should be identified and resolved before initiating treatments with electroculture.

OVERVIEW OF ELECTROCULTURE APPLICATION IN HYDROPONICS

Electroculture in hydroponics refers to using small electrical currents through the nutrient solution in hydroponics systems to stimulate plant growth and enhance overall plant health. Electric current is usually applied through electrodes submerged within the solution; intensity and frequency can then be managed for maximum effectiveness.

Advantages Of Electroculture In Hydroponics

- Increased plant Growth: Electroculture can facilitate plant growth within hydroponics systems, leading to larger and healthier plants.

- Improved Nutrient Uptake: Electrical current can help plants better absorb nutrients, improving their overall health.

- Resistance To Pests and Diseases: Electroculture can help plants to be more resistant to pests and diseases by improving their overall health, making them more resistant to pests and diseases.

- Reduced need for fertilizers: Electroculture's ability to improve nutrient uptake and plant growth reduces the need for additional fertilizers in hydroponic systems, thus cutting costs significantly.

Key Considerations For Electroculture In Hydroponics

- Optimized Electrical Frequency and Intensity: For optimal results, both the frequency and intensity of electrical current should be carefully managed to achieve desired outcomes. Too much electricity could potentially harm plants while too little might not have any significant effect.

- Electrode Placement: Care must be taken when positioning electrodes within a hydroponics system to ensure an even distribution of current that doesn't harm plants.

- Timing and Duration of Electroculture Treatment: Care must be taken when scheduling electroculture treatments to minimize overexposure to electric current, which could prove damaging to plants.

- Safety Considerations: Electroculture in hydroponics should always put safety first. All electrical components should be installed and grounded properly, and any potential hazards must be identified and addressed before initiating electroculture treatments.

Challenges And Limitations Of ElectroCulture In Hydroponics

- High cost of electroculture equipment and maintenance: Electroculture equipment can be an expensive investment for hydroponic growers. Initial investments may include electrodes, controllers, and monitoring equipment as well as ongoing maintenance costs that could prove prohibitive to growth.

- Lack of Understanding the Long-term Effects of Electroculture: Electroculture has shown promising short-term results; however, research on its long-term impact remains limited in hydroponic systems. Potential impacts on plant health, nutrient uptake, and productivity must first be fully comprehended before electroculture can be widely adopted.

- Electroculture may harm plant health and productivity: Hydroponic systems using electroculture have the potential to negatively affect plant health and productivity, as excessive electrical current could harm plants by disrupting their growth cycle and potentially harming overall system health and productivity.

- Regulation hurdles: Electroculture in hydroponics may present challenges when used with equipment that isn't already approved for agricultural purposes, which requires growers to navigate regulations and obtain permits before beginning this practice in their hydroponic systems.

FUTURE RESEARCH DIRECTIONS IN ELECTROCULTURE AQUAPONICS AND HYDROPONICS

Investigation into optimal conditions for electroculture therapy:

Future research should aim at identifying optimal electroculture treatment conditions, including frequency, duration, and intensity of the electrical current. This will enable scientists to discover the most efficient way of using electroculture in aquaponics and hydroponics environments.

Ascertaining the effects of electroculture on plant growth and development:

Further research must be conducted to understand the specific effects of electroculture on plant growth and development, including how electrical current influences plant physiology and metabolism.

Study of the long-term impacts of electroculture on fish health and plant productivity:

Electroculture has shown promise in short-term studies, yet more in-depth analyses are necessary to fully comprehend its long-term effects on fish health and productivity over time. Such investigations can identify any risks or adverse side effects caused by electroculture in aquaponics or hydroponics systems.

Evaluation of electroculture systems used for hydroponic and aquaponic farming:

Future research should investigate electroculture's application in various hydroponic and aquaponic systems, including those using various nutrient solutions, plant varieties, and fish species. This will allow scientists to better determine its applicability and potential benefits in various agricultural settings.

Conclusion

Electroculture shows great promise as a sustainable and effective means for improving plant growth and nutrient uptake within both aquaponics and hydroponics systems. Although there may be drawbacks associated with this technology, such as its high equipment and maintenance costs and limited understanding of long-term effects, its many potential benefits could outweigh these obstacles and drawbacks, including reduced use of chemicals and improved microbial activity. Further research is required to optimize electroculture treatment conditions, assess its long-term impacts on plant and fish health, and measure its efficacy in different agricultural settings. Adopting electroculture in aquaponics or hydroponics has the potential to transform sustainable agriculture practices while contributing to more environmentally-friendly food production systems.

ELECTROCULTURE IN FORESTRY

Forestry is the science-based management of forests for human use and environmental sustainability. This includes studying forest ecosystems, growing and managing trees both commercially and non-commercially, as well as conserving forest resources.

Forestry encompasses numerous activities, such as tree planting, forest management, timber harvesting, wildlife conservation, and recreation planning. Furthermore, forestry includes managing fires, pests, and diseases while also restoring degraded forests.

Forestry assists forests in providing crucial resources such as timber, non-timber forest products, and clean water. Forests also support biodiversity by providing habitats for wildlife and helping regulate Earth's climate; plus they can be important cultural and recreational assets that offer hiking, camping, and other outdoor recreation opportunities.

Effective forest management ensures the long-term health and sustainability of forest ecosystems, calling upon sound scientific principles, careful planning, and clear communications between forest managers, stakeholders, and the public.

Electroculture can revolutionize our approach to managing and maintaining forests. Through electricity, we can increase soil health, reduce pests and diseases, increase yields from tree crops, and improve yields in tree farms.

Electroculture rests on the principle that plants respond to electromagnetic radiation similar to sunlight, with different wavelengths having various effects on the growth and development of plants. By manipulating the electromagnetic spectrum we can increase plant growth while improving health.

Electroculture techniques are an essential tool in forestry, including electromagnetic field application, electrostatic precipitation, electro-irrigation, electro-organic cultivation, and electrolysis for soil improvement. Each of these utilizes electricity differently to achieve results.

Electroculture offers many advantages for forestry, including improved growth and yield, reduced pests and diseases, soil improvement/remediation/conservation/management as well as water conservation/management. Unfortunately, Electroculture also presents some obstacles and limitations, including its high initial costs, limited research into long-term effects as well as any negative side effects it might have on the environment.

Electroculture has already proven its worth in forestry, with several successful case studies attesting to its promise for improving forest health and productivity. As more research in this area continues, Electroculture could become an integral tool of sustainable forest management.

ELECTROCULTURE TECHNIQUES IN FORESTRY

Electroculture techniques use electricity to manipulate electromagnetic fields and boost plant growth. Forestry involves various techniques for improving soil health, and yields and decreasing pests and diseases.

- Electromagnetic Field Application: Electromagnetic field applications to plants to promote growth and development are an effective strategy, exposing plants to specific frequencies of electromagnetic radiation that can improve photosynthesis, nutrient absorption, and root development.

- Electrostatic Precipitation: Electrostatic precipitation is an electrical charge-based technique used to attract and remove airborne pollutants such as smoke and industrial emissions, that may harm plant growth and development. Foresters can utilize this practice to help eliminate airborne pollutants which might adversely impact tree health and development.

- Electro-irrigation: Electro-irrigation involves applying an electrical charge to irrigation water to increase soil conductivity and facilitate plant nutrition absorption. Furthermore, this technique reduces water usage by increasing efficiency in its use thereby decreasing the required amounts for irrigation.

- Electro-organic Cultivation: Electro-organic cultivation is an electrical cultivation technique designed to increase soil health and increase plant growth. The application of low-voltage electrical charges helps enhance fertility and boost nutrient levels within the soil.

- Electrolysis for Soil Improvement: Electrolysis involves applying an electrical current to the soil to eliminate pollutants and enhance the structure, helping remediate polluted areas or restoring degraded sites. It may also be used for remediating contaminated sites and improving health in degraded locations.

Each of these Electroculture techniques can be applied in forestry to enhance forest health and productivity. The choice of technique is based on the specific goals of the forestry management program and the particular challenges facing the forest ecosystem.

BENEFITS OF ELECTROCULTURE IN FORESTRY

Electroculture techniques provide various benefits to forestry management programs. These benefits include:

- Improved Growth and Yield: Electroculture can boost plant growth and development, resulting in faster and more robust growth in tree crops. This leads to higher timber yields and more productive forests.

- Reducing Pests and Diseases: Electroculture techniques can strengthen a plant's natural defense mechanisms to make it less susceptible to damage from pests and diseases, thus decreasing reliance on chemical pesticides and fungicides - leading to more sustainable, eco-friendly forestry management practices.

- Soil Improvement and Remediation: Electroculture can provide several beneficial solutions for soil improvement and remediation, from improving health and fixing contaminated areas to restoring degraded ecosystems and supporting sustainable forestry practices by increasing fertility and strengthening the structure.

- Water Conservation and Management: Electro-irrigation techniques can increase the efficiency of water use in forest management programs. Electroculture reduces irrigation water requirements by improving soil conductivity and increasing plant nutrient uptake, leading to more sustainable practices that promote better soil conductivity and uptake of nutrients by plants.

Electroculture provides many benefits to forest management programs, such as increased productivity, reduced environmental impact, and enhanced sustainability. As research in this field continues, Electroculture has become a relevant tool for sustainable forestry management.

CHALLENGES AND LIMITATIONS OF ELECTROCULTURE IN FORESTRY

Although Electroculture provides various benefits to forestry management programs, there are also some challenges and limitations linked to this technique. These include:

- High Initial Cost: The equipment and technology for Electroculture can be costly, making it difficult for smaller forestry management programs to implement this technique.

- Limited Research on Long-Term Effects: Although case studies prove the potential of Electroculture for forest management, research on its long-term effects remains scarce - making it hard to fully grasp both risks and benefits associated with using it in this environment.

- Possible Negative Impacts on the Environment: Although Electroculture provides various benefits to forestry management programs, there is also potential for negative impacts on the environment. For instance, electro-irrigation may improve soil salinity levels over time, resulting in decreased soil fertility and reduced plant growth. Moreover, electromagnetic fields may harm wildlife and other organisms in the forest ecosystem.

In conclusion, although Electroculture provides various benefits to forestry management programs, there are also various challenges and limitations linked to this technique. These should be thoroughly considered and tackled when implementing Electroculture in forestry management programs to ensure that the technique is safely and sustainably applied.

CASE STUDIES OF ELECTROCULTURE IN FORESTRY

There are various successful case studies of Electroculture in forestry from different regions and contexts. These case studies prove the potential of Electroculture in enhancing forest health and productivity. Some examples include:

- Electro-irrigation in a pine forest in Spain: Researchers applied an electrical charge to irrigation water in a pine forest in Spain, which increased the tree growth by 25% compared to trees that were not treated. The study also discovered that Electro-irrigation reduced water use by 20%.

Researchers applied electromagnetic radiation at a specific frequency to a eucalyptus plantation in Brazil, resulting in 30% higher tree height and 12% larger stem diameter than trees not treated.

Electro-organic cultivation in a degraded forest in India: Researchers applied low voltage electrical charges to degraded forest soil in India, increasing soil fertility and increasing plant species within it. This approach decreased chemical fertilizer requirements while improving overall forest ecosystem health.

Electroculture can improve forest health and productivity in different regions and contexts, yet much remains unknown about its long-term impacts and how best it can be tailored for specific forest ecosystems. These case studies demonstrate this potential.

Case studies highlight the significance of planning and implementing Electroculture techniques carefully, including ongoing monitoring and research to ensure their safety and effectiveness. Further investigation should focus on understanding its risks and benefits within forest management programs as well as ways to optimize it for various forest ecosystems.

Conclusion

Electroculture is an innovative technique that has been useful in forestry management programs. This technique includes applying electrical fields to plants, soil, and water to enhance forest health and productivity. Electroculture techniques such as electromagnetic field application, electro-irrigation, electro-organic cultivation, and electrolysis for soil improvement can boost growth and yield, reduce pests and diseases, enhance soil fertility and remediation, and conserve water.

Despite the benefits, there are also challenges and limitations linked to Electroculture in forestry management programs. These involve the high initial cost, limited research on long-term effects, and potential negative impacts on the environment. Henceforth, thorough planning, implementation of Electroculture techniques, and ongoing monitoring and research will ensure that this technique is used safely and sustainably in forestry management programs.

Successful case studies of Electroculture in forestry from different regions and contexts prove the potential of this technique in enhancing forest health and productivity. Yet much remains to be discovered about the long-term impacts and optimization strategies for Electroculture within various forest ecosystems.

In conclusion, Electroculture can provide many potential advantages to forest management programs, with further research to understand both risks and rewards of this technique, including creating best practices to ensure its safe implementation.

PART 5: BENEFITS AND CHALLENGES OF ELECTROCULTURE

Electroculture's benefits include reduced dependence on chemical fertilizers and pesticides, improved plant health and yield, as well as stronger resistance against environmental stressors such as drought or disease.

Electroculture can help increase agricultural productivity and sustainability in areas with poor soil quality or limited access to water resources, yet this technique also faces several obstacles; initial investments required for Electroculture equipment may make using it challenging for small-scale farmers.

However, no scientific research exists on the long-term impacts of electrical stimulation on plant health and the environment. More studies should fully comprehend its risks and benefits to establish guidelines for its safe and effective usage - which we will discuss here in this chapter.

IMPROVED PLANT GROWTH AND YIELDS

One of the benefits of Electroculture is improving plant growth and yields.

The electrical current applied to plants during Electroculture can boost plant growth and increase the plant's nutrient absorption from the soil. This leads to stronger, healthier plants with better root development for increased yields.

Electroculture can increase photosynthesis efficiency in plants, which is the process by which they convert sunlight to energy, leading to faster growth and higher yields.

In conclusion, Electroculture can help farmers increase plant growth and yields, making this form of agriculture invaluable to increasing crop production and yields. Results will depend on factors like plant type, soil conditions, application of electrical current, and length of exposure time.

REDUCED NEED FOR FERTILIZERS AND PESTICIDES

Electroculture offers many advantages over other methods for growing plants, one being reduced fertilizers and pesticide use. Electroculture has become a sustainable and cost-effective means of cultivating crops in areas where chemical fertilizers or pesticides may be too costly or harmful to the environment to use effectively.

Applying weak electrical currents to soil or plants can create an environment suitable for plant growth and health, leading to stronger, healthier plants that are less vulnerable to diseases and pests - thus decreasing or even eliminating the need for chemical pesticides.

Chemical pesticides can cause significant environmental harm, to both wildlife and humans alike. Overuse of pesticides may contaminate soil and water supplies as well as harm beneficial insects like pollinators. Furthermore, overusing them may develop resistant pests making control harder over time.

Electroculture provides an eco-friendly and sustainable alternative to chemical pesticides. Electroculture reduces chemical treatments by strengthening plants' natural defense mechanisms against disease and pests; in addition, its electrical currents leave no chemical residues behind that could erode soil health or increase environmental pollution.

Electroculture offers another effective solution to reduce chemical fertilizer needs and associated environmental costs, including negative impacts. By improving soil health and increasing the availability of nutrients without synthetic fertilizers, electroculture can facilitate plant growth and development without artificial additives - thus helping reduce costs related to chemical fertilizers while lessening their negative impacts on the environment.

Chemical fertilizers can damage both soil health and the environment in many ways. Overuse of fertilizers can lead to soil acidification, depleted nutrient reserves, and increased greenhouse gas emissions. Furthermore, excess nutrients from fertilizers may seep into nearby waterways causing harmful algal blooms and other environmental problems.
ElectroCulture can offer an eco-friendly farming approach by minimizing chemical fertilizers and pesticide use, helping maintain soil health while decreasing environmental pollution levels and supporting healthier food production.

Electroculture offers many benefits to farmers and the environment alike, including reduced fertilizers and pesticide needs, reduced chemical treatments' negative impacts on human health, as well as creation more natural conditions for plant growth compared to traditional farming practices; it could therefore serve as an excellent tool to create a more sustainable future in agriculture.

IMPROVED SOIL HEALTH

Improved soil health is one of the benefits of Electroculture. Soil health is crucial to the success of agriculture, providing essential nutrients, water, and physical support to plants for healthy development. Unfortunately, certain conventional farming practices such as tiling, using chemical fertilizers and pesticides inappropriately, or monoculture cropping can compromise soil health over time, leading to degradation and eventually erosion.

Electroculture can boost soil health by stimulating beneficial soil microorganisms, increasing nutrient availability, and minimizing soil compaction. Applying low electrical currents to the soil can promote the growth and activity of microorganisms such as bacteria and fungi that break down organic matter while cycling nutrients throughout. This ultimately increases organic matter for improved soil structure, water retention, and availability.

Electroculture can also reduce soil compaction, an issue commonly encountered in intensive agricultural practices. Soil compaction reduces air, water, and nutrients moving freely through the soil resulting in poor plant growth and lower crop yields. Electric currents used in Electroculture break up soil particles to enhance the structural support of the soil to alleviate compaction while simultaneously improving soil health and improving plant growth.

Improved soil health is also key in mitigating agriculture's detrimental environmental impacts, including soil erosion, water quality improvements, and biodiversity enhancement. Furthermore, healthier soils help mitigate climate change by storing carbon in their core, limiting greenhouse gas emissions, and boosting fertility.

Electroculture offers several benefits to both farmers and the environment, including improved soil health. Electroculture can improve soil health and support sustainable agriculture by encouraging beneficial soil microorganisms, increasing nutrient availability, and minimizing soil compaction - leading to increased crop yields with reduced chemical fertilizers/pesticide usage as well as more environmentally friendly farming techniques.

POTENTIAL FOR GREENHOUSE GAS REDUCTION

Electroculture provides one of the greatest potential benefits in terms of greenhouse gas reduction: carbon dioxide (CO_2), methane (CH_4), and nitrous oxide (N_2O) are greenhouse gasses responsible for climate change by trapping heat within Earth's atmosphere - contributing significantly to global warming. Agriculture accounts for many greenhouse gas emissions via synthetic fertilizers, pesticides, and machinery emissions which contribute a large proportion.

Electroculture can help reduce greenhouse gas emissions by encouraging healthier soil and plant growth to store carbon in the soil and limit synthetic fertilizer use. Electrical currents applied to either soil or plants can promote beneficial soil microorganisms that break down organic matter into carbon storage sites for improved fertility, water retention, nutrient availability, and climate change mitigation while mitigating climate change by decreasing CO_2 in the atmosphere.

Electroculture can also reduce greenhouse gas emissions through reduced use of synthetic fertilizers, which are an energy-intensive production and transport process. By improving soil health and increasing nutrient availability, electroculture reduces synthetic fertilizer usage for crop production to help lower GHG emissions.

Electroculture farming practices can increase crop diversity while mitigating the negative consequences of monoculture cropping which leads to soil erosion, reduced biodiversity, and increased greenhouse gas emissions. Electroculture creates an eco-friendly farming approach by supporting healthier soil conditions and plant growth while simultaneously lowering greenhouse gas emissions.

Electroculture can help reduce greenhouse gas emissions. Electroculture can combat climate change while providing a more sustainable approach to agriculture through the promotion of healthier soil and plant growth, reduced use of synthetic fertilizers, and greater crop diversity. Yet more research needs to be completed before fully understanding Electroculture and its effect on greenhouse gas emissions.

SAFETY CONCERNS OF ELECTROCULTURE

Safety concerns are one of the challenges of Electroculture. Agriculture employing electric currents presents several safety concerns, particularly around electric shock risks. Farmers and workers must exercise great caution when using electroculture technology so as not to cause injury or even death.

As previously discussed, one of the primary safety concerns associated with Electroculture is electric shock risk. Electrical currents used on plants or soil could pose the possibility of electric shock for farmers or workers using the equipment; further exacerbated by environmental conditions like rain and damp soil which increase the conductivity of electrical currents.

Farmers and workers using Electroculture must take appropriate precautions to minimize the risk of electric shock, such as wearing protective clothing and using insulated equipment, as well as following installation and operating procedures properly. Furthermore, regular checks of this equipment should be undertaken by farmers to ensure its functionality as intended and to replace any damaged or worn components immediately.

Another safety risk associated with Electroculture is fire or explosion. Electroculture involves electrical currents which generate heat that can ignite flammable materials or gasses. To decrease this risk, appropriate equipment and operating procedures should be used, along with keeping equipment away from flammable materials while using non-combustible materials in the construction of equipment.

Electroculture may pose an increased threat to wildlife, particularly birds that may be drawn toward electrical currents. This can cause bird strikes or electrocution and harm the local wildlife populations. Therefore, farmers and workers must take appropriate measures to prevent wildlife from getting closer to the electrical currents, such as using bird deterrents or installing equipment in areas where wildlife would hardly visit.

In conclusion, safety concerns are one of the challenges of Electroculture. The use of electrical currents in agriculture poses a potential risk of electric shock, fire, or explosion, and a risk to wildlife. Farmers and workers must take appropriate safety measures when using Electroculture to prevent injury or death and to reduce harm to wildlife populations. Farmers should adhere to proper installation and operating procedures, constantly inspect and maintain the equipment, and use proper protective clothing and insulated equipment.

CONTROVERSIES AND SKEPTICISM

Electroculture is a controversial topic that uses electrical energy to boost plant growth and increase crop yield. Therefore, controversies and skepticism are some of the major challenges experienced in the adoption and implementation of electroculture.

Electroculture has generated considerable controversy due to a lack of scientific proof supporting claims made by its proponents, potential adverse environmental consequences, and safety considerations in using electrical energy in agriculture.

Additionally, critics argue that electroculture is just an elaborate marketing gimmick designed to take advantage of farmers and consumers without providing any substantial scientific foundation. They highlighted that most of the claims made by electroculture advocates are not backed up by peer-reviewed scientific studies or data.

The controversy surrounding electroculture has created skepticism among farmers, agricultural experts, and policymakers, which has made it difficult to gain widespread acceptance and adoption. Despite this, some believe that electroculture can revolutionize agriculture and tackle some of the challenges experienced in traditional farming methods.

In conclusion, the controversies and skepticism surrounding electroculture show the need for further research and investigation to determine its potential benefits and drawbacks. Additionally, more education will help farmers and stakeholders to make informed decisions regarding electroculture use in agriculture.

TECHNICAL AND ECONOMIC CHALLENGES

Electroculture can be an immensely rewarding agricultural technique that increases crop yields while reducing dependence on traditional farming techniques. Yet before its widespread deployment can occur, several technical and economic challenges must first be met head-on.

One of the primary technical challenges associated with electroculture is designing reliable and efficient electrical systems that foster plant growth. To do this, electrodes and transformers require specialist knowledge to operate effectively and can be expensive to maintain.

Apart from technical challenges, electroculture also experiences economic challenges that must be overcome. One of the main economic challenges is the high cost of implementing electroculture systems, which can be a major barrier for small-scale farmers and those in developing countries.

Furthermore, there are no standardized methods for measuring the effectiveness of electroculture, which makes it hard to determine the return on investment for farmers. Farmers may find it difficult to justify the initial investment needed to implement electroculture systems.

Lastly, electroculture also experiences regulatory and policy challenges, especially regarding safety and environmental concerns. These concerns may result in increased regulatory oversight, which can further increase the cost of implementing electroculture systems.

Electroculture offers many potential advantages; however, its wide adoption into agriculture still presents many technical and financial hurdles that must be surmounted before widespread implementation can occur. Overcoming these hurdles requires ongoing research and development efforts involving collaboration among researchers, farmers, policymakers, industry professionals, etc.

PART 6: FUTURE DIRECTIONS IN ELECTROCULTURE

RESEARCH NEEDS AND OPPORTUNITIES

Electroculture is a field of research that investigates how electrical energy affects plant growth and development. Although some work has already been completed in this area, there remain unanswered questions as well as opportunities for further investigation.

Electroculture research is an intriguing area of investigation with the potential to increase crop yields and enhance plant health. Studies have demonstrated how electrical current can accelerate plant growth rates, boost nutrient uptake rates and provide enhanced protection from pests and disease.

Another area of research is using electroculture to improve plant-based medicinal compounds. Several plants consist of compounds with medicinal properties, and there is proof to suggest that applying electrical energy to these plants will boost the concentration of these compounds.

Electroculture offers an opportunity for sustainable agriculture practices. Electroculture can improve soil health while decreasing environmental pollution by eliminating chemical fertilizers and pesticides from use in farming practices.

To advance electroculture research, researchers must develop more efficient means of examining how electrical energy affects plant life. They also need to conduct large-scale trials to know the optimal electrical parameters for various plant species and growing conditions.

Lastly, it's important to develop practical applications for electroculture in agriculture. This involves creating cost-effective methods for providing electrical energy to crops and adding electroculture into existing agricultural practices.

In conclusion, electroculture is an interesting area of research with several opportunities for further investigation. By investigating the potential of electrical energy to boost plant growth and enhance agricultural practices, researchers can help to develop more sustainable and efficient farming practices.

TECHNOLOGICAL DEVELOPMENTS

In electroculture, many technological developments should shape the future of the field. Some of these developments include:

Smart Sensors

Smart sensors are one of the latest technological developments in electroculture. They serve to monitor and optimize plant growth by providing real-time information about soil moisture levels, temperature, and other environmental variables.

These sensors collect information that allows farmers to adjust watering and fertilization schedules for optimal plant growth. If soil moisture levels fall too low, for instance, sensors can notify farmers to water their plants again; or if temperatures become excessively hot or cold respectively, sensors notify them so that climate control systems can be altered accordingly.

Smart sensors provide one of the primary benefits to farmers: helping them make more informed decisions regarding watering and fertilizing crops - helping reduce water consumption while increasing crop yields. In addition, smart sensors can detect areas on farms experiencing environmental stress so farmers can act before it harms plants.

Smart sensors are an indispensable asset for farmers who seek to increase crop yields while decreasing environmental impact. By providing real-time environmental data, smart sensors enable farmers to make better-informed decisions and achieve improved results.

Precision Agriculture

Precision agriculture is a modern form of electroculture that allows farmers to precisely manage the amount and timing of inputs like water, fertilizers, and pesticides for each crop. Precision farming utilizes sensors, global positioning systems (GPS), and other advanced technologies to monitor soil conditions, weather patterns, and plant growth patterns in real-time.

Precision agriculture allows farmers to apply inputs only where and when needed, thus minimizing waste and environmental impact. For instance, using GPS data, precision agriculture allows a farmer to identify areas in his/her farm that are experiencing water stress so he/she can apply water only there instead of across an entire field.

Precision agriculture offers farmers another key benefit - increasing crop yields. By helping identify areas on their farm that may be underperforming and offering real-time data on soil moisture levels, temperature, and other environmental variables - precision agriculture helps farmers improve yields significantly.

In conclusion, Precision agriculture represents an emerging technology in electroculture that could significantly change how farmers farm. Precision agriculture offers farmers opportunities to maximize yields while decreasing waste and environmental impact by providing real-time data and precise control over inputs.

Artificial Intelligence

Artificial Intelligence (AI) is the field of computer science that creates intelligent machines capable of performing tasks that usually require human intelligence, including learning, problem-solving, and decision-making. A subfield of AI called machine learning employs algorithms that learn patterns in data to make predictions or decisions based on them.

AI and machine learning technologies provide farmers with an effective tool for analyzing vast amounts of agricultural data such as plant growth, soil health issues, weather patterns, and any other variables influencing crop production. By analyzing this information, AI algorithms can uncover patterns that enable more informed decisions to be made regarding planting, fertilization, irrigation, and pest management practices.

While AI and machine learning can offer valuable insights for farmers practicing Electroculture, the technique itself is not directly associated with AI. Yet, AI helps to analyze data from Electroculture experiments to discover the most effective electrical stimuli and optimize the technique for increased crop yield and soil health.

Genetic Engineering

Genetic engineering is a technique for manipulating an organism's genetic material to add or alter characteristics or modify existing ones. Recombinant DNA technology allows this alteration by adding, deleting, or changing specific genes in their genetic code.

Electroculture requires genetic engineering for optimal production. Genetic engineers use specific genes added into plant genomes to modify how their responses to electrical stimulation affect yields, making plants more responsive to electroculture methods and yields.

Genetic engineering allows genetic engineers to introduce specific genes which promote root growth or increase the production of certain hormones in response to electrical stimuli, increasing nutrient absorption and yield for increased crop yields.

Genetic engineering can also assist in creating crops more resistant to pests and diseases, thus decreasing the need for harmful chemicals like pesticides - improving sustainability while decreasing the environmental impact of farming practices.

In conclusion, Genetic engineering can be an excellent way to boost the efficacy of Electroculture by creating crops specifically tailored for this technique and more resistant to pests and diseases.

Vertical Farming

Vertical farming is a method of growing crops in urban environments with limited lands in vertically stacked layers through artificial lighting and controlled environmental conditions. This technique can improve the yield per unit area of land, minimize water consumption, and offer fresh produce in urban areas.

In the context of Electroculture, vertical farming can be an effective tool to apply the Electroculture technique in an urban environment. Vertical farming enables more efficient use of space, as multiple layers of crops can be cultivated in a single building or structure. This can minimize the amount of land needed for farming and improve the number of crops to be grown in a limited area.

Also, vertical farming can offer a controlled environment for plants, which can be customized to improve the Electroculture technique. By controlling factors such as temperature, humidity, and light intensity, the electrical stimuli channeled to the plants can be optimized for maximum effect. This can boost plant growth and higher yields.

Vertical farming can also be integrated with other technological developments in Electroculture, such as artificial intelligence and automation. Through AI and machine learning algorithms that analyze plant growth data and environmental conditions, electroculture techniques can be optimized in real time for every specific crop.

In conclusion, vertical farming is a technological development of Electroculture that can boost the efficiency of crop production and make the technique useful in urban environments. Vertical farming helps to increase the potential of the Electroculture technique by offering a controlled environment and optimizing the electrical stimuli delivered to plants.

Hydroponics

Hydroponics is an efficient way to grow plants without using soil, using instead a nutrient-rich water solution as their medium. It is a technology that is a component of Electroculture.

In hydroponics, plants are usually grown in a soilless medium such as perlite, coconut coir, or rock wool. The plants' roots are then suspended in a nutrient solution that has all the needed minerals and nutrients needed for growth. This solution is frequently circulated through the growing medium so that the plants get a regular supply of nutrients.

Electroculture technologies can be added to hydroponics systems to further improve plant growth. Researchers have recently revealed that applying a low-level electric current to hydroponic plants can significantly accelerate root growth, and enhance nutrient uptake and overall plant health. Furthermore, electroculture techniques such as pulsed electromagnetic fields (PEMFs) and plasma treatments have proven their efficacy in increasing crop yields in hydroponic systems.

Hydroponics is an amazing technology, offering numerous advantages over soil-based agriculture. By adding electroculture techniques, hydroponic systems can further increase efficiency and effectiveness for increased crop yields and higher-quality produce.

In conclusion, Electroculture's future lies in its combination of technologies and emphasis on eco-friendly agricultural practices that meet growing food demands while decreasing environmental impact.

POLICY IMPLICATIONS OF ELECTROCULTURE

As with any new technology, there are policy implications associated with electroculture that must be carefully considered to ensure its safe and responsible usage. These actions by governments and policymakers to promote its adoption while assuring its safe implementation can help promote its adoption while benefiting both farmers and the environment alike.

Here are three policy implications of electroculture:

- Government Subsidies and Incentives to Promote Electroculture Adoption in Farmers: Governments can offer financial support and incentives for farmers interested in adopting electroculture, such as grants, loans, tax breaks, or any other form of financial assistance. Such measures can reduce the financial strain associated with adopting new agricultural technologies while encouraging their use by encouraging their adoption of electroculture by farmers.

- Regulating electroculture to ensure safety and prevent negative environmental impacts: Governments can regulate electroculture to protect both humans and the environment from its potentially harmful impacts, including standards for using equipment, electrical safety protocols, and measures to avoid soil or water contamination. Likewise, regulations may address any negative biodiversity impacts to ensure sustainable implementation of electroculture.

- Integration of Electroculture Into Sustainable Agriculture Policies and Practices: Governments can incorporate electroculture into sustainable agriculture policies and practices to reduce environmental impact, conserve natural resources, and increase farming communities' economic viability. By including electroculture within such policies, farmers will gain access to information and resources necessary for adopting and sustainably implementing electroculture technology.

Overall, these policy implications can help foster the adoption of electroculture as a sustainable and cost-effective agriculture practice.

CHALLENGES TO IMPLEMENTING ELECTROCULTURE

Electroculture implementation poses various challenges, with three major ones being:

- Initial Investment Costs: Electroculture requires significant initial investments in equipment and technology such as electrodes, generators, and controllers - these costs may pose an obstacle for farmers with limited financial resources - not to mention ongoing maintenance and repair expenses that could become prohibitively expensive over time.

- Lack of Awareness and Education About Electroculture among Farmers: Many farmers may be unfamiliar with electroculture and its potential advantages; without the knowledge, skills, or confidence necessary to implement the technology effectively, or unwillingness to adopt unfamiliar technologies due to uncertainty of risks/benefits involved, many may remain ignorant to its existence and its advantages.

- Electroculture Research and Development Gaps: While electroculture has proven its efficacy in improving plant growth and yield, more research needs to be conducted in this field to understand optimal conditions, potential risks and benefits associated with its use, training programs to help farmers adopt and implement electroculture effectively and more education programs in this regard are required.

Overall, these challenges highlight the need for additional research, education, and support to assist farmers with adopting and implementing electroculture efficiently. Tackling these issues requires collaboration among farmers, researchers, policymakers, and other stakeholders ensuring electroculture can be implemented sustainably and successfully.

CASE STUDIES OF ELECTROCULTURE IMPLEMENTATION

Electroculture is an increasingly controversial agricultural technique involving the application of low-voltage electrical current to soil or plant tissues to stimulate plant growth and increase crop yields. While anecdotal evidence exists to support electroculture's effects on plant growth, no scientific data exist that directly supports its effectiveness; nonetheless, case studies of its implementation have been documented in scientific publications.

Electroculture and Wine Grape Production

In 2008, a vineyard in California implemented an electroculture system to see if it would enhance the growth and yield of their wine grape crops. The system involved applying low-level electrical current through metal rods placed into the ground; they reported some positive effects such as increased leaf size and improved sugar content. Unfortunately, results weren't consistent among all grape varieties they grew and this experiment couldn't be considered scientifically rigorous.

The vineyard utilized a commercial electroculture system of electrodes placed into the soil around vines. Each electrode was connected to a power supply that delivered low-voltage electric current to ensure safe conditions for plant life. Voltage and current levels were regularly monitored to remain within safe limits for their plants.

The vineyard reported that their electroculture system appeared to enhance the growth and yield of certain grape varieties, but not others. Their findings suggested it worked best when used on healthy vines with adequate nutrient and water supply as well as increasing sugar content - an integral factor of wine quality.

However, the results of this study should be interpreted with caution as they rely on anecdotal evidence and have yet to be scientifically verified. Further rigorous scientific research needs to be conducted to ascertain any possible benefits electroculture could bring to wine grape production.

Electroculture and Potato Production

Harry R. Steward was a UK farmer who implemented electroculture on his potato crop fields during the late 1970s. Steward claimed that electroculture produced larger and healthier potatoes; even patenting his design for an electroculture system. Unfortunately, no independent evidence supports his claims; consequently, the scientific community remains skeptical of electroculture as an agricultural technique.

Steward's electroculture system consisted of electrodes placed around potato plants and connected to a power supply, which provided low-level electric current. He claimed this electrical current stimulated their growth, leading to larger and healthier potatoes.

Although Steward's claims have yet to be scientifically verified, several scientific studies have explored the benefits of electroculture on potato production. One such investigation published in 1986's Journal of Agricultural Science found no statistical difference in yield or quality between crops grown with or without electroculture.

Another study published in 1992's Journal of Plant Nutrition examined the effects of electroculture on the growth and yield of potato plants grown in greenhouse conditions. They discovered no discernible change to either growth or yield from this form of cultivation.

Overall, electroculture has only been successfully utilized in potato production based on some anecdotal reports; unfortunately, no scientific data supports its efficiency.

Electroculture and Hydroponic Vegetable Production

Australian researchers conducted a study assessing the effects of electroculture on hydroponic lettuce plant growth and yield. They discovered that applying low-level electrical current to their nutrient solution caused significant increases in both plant growth and yield.

The study used a commercial electroculture system with electrodes immersed in nutrient solution and connected to a power source that provided low-level electrical current for electrode immersion. Researchers observed that increasing plant uptake increased yield and speeded growth rates and yields.

This research also found that electroculture had no adverse impacts on either the quality or taste of lettuce grown hydroponically, suggesting it might be an effective means of increasing hydroponic vegetable production.

While this study offers evidence to back the benefits of electroculture on hydroponic vegetable production, it should be remembered that its results come from one experiment alone and should be replicated elsewhere to verify their reliability.

Electroculture and Wheat Production

In 2019, Pakistan conducted a study to explore the effects of electroculture on wheat crop growth and yield. For the research project, a commercial electroculture system with electrodes embedded into the soil around wheat plants was utilized, with each electrode connected to its power supply that distributed low-level electrical current to provide low-level electric current throughout.

This study found that electroculture systems produced significant increases in wheat yield, producing up to 25% more wheat in treated plots compared to control plots. Researchers also noticed an increase in root length and biomass of wheat plants suggesting it may have stimulated root growth.

Although this study provides evidence of electroculture's potential benefits on wheat production, it must be remembered that its findings rely on one experiment only and must be replicated elsewhere to verify their reliability.

Electroculture and Tomato Production

Egypt conducted a research project in 2018 to study the effects of electroculture on tomato production. A commercial electroculture system consisted of electrodes placed throughout the soil surrounding tomato plants that were connected to a power source that delivered low-voltage electrical current to each electrode and finally to an electroculture power supply that provided current.

The study revealed that electroculture systems had a profound impact on tomato yield, producing up to 24% more tomatoes in treated plots compared to control plots. Researchers observed an increase in the chlorophyll content of tomato leaves due to electroculture systems indicating improved photosynthetic activity.

Although this study provides some evidence in support of electroculture's potential benefits in tomato production, it should be remembered that its conclusions are dependent on only one experiment and must be replicated elsewhere to establish reliability.

Electroculture and Strawberry Production

Italy conducted a 2015 study to study the effects of electroculture on strawberry production. For this research, they utilized a commercial electroculture system composed of electrodes placed throughout the soil surrounding strawberry plants connected to a power supply that supplied low-level electrical current to their electrical current supply system.

In their research, researchers discovered that electroculture systems led to a substantial increase in strawberry yield; treated plots produced up to 40% more strawberries than controls. They also noticed an increase in the size, weight, and sugar content of the strawberries produced under electroculture conditions.

While this study provides some evidence for the benefits of electroculture on strawberry production, it must be remembered that its results come from only one experiment and must be confirmed in other settings to verify their reliability.

Electroculture and Lettuce Production

In South Korea, researchers in 2012 investigated the effects of electroculture on lettuce production. For the research, a commercial electroculture system with electrodes immersed in nutrient solution in which lettuce was growing was employed to conduct this investigation; each electrode was connected to its power supply providing low levels of electric current to keep its potential at maximum.

The study concluded that electroculture systems led to a significant increase in lettuce yield, producing up to 22% more lettuce in treated plots compared with their control counterparts. Furthermore, researchers noted increased nutrient uptake as well as antioxidant content from this system.

Although this study provides some evidence in support of electroculture's potential benefits on lettuce production, it should be remembered that its results come from only one experiment and need to be repeated elsewhere to establish reliability.

Electroculture and Bean Production

Mexico conducted a 2013 study to examine the effects of electroculture on bean production. They used a commercial electroculture system consisting of electrodes buried around bean plants connected to an electrical current source supplying low levels of electricity into the soil.

The study's researchers observed that electroculture systems caused an impressive increase in bean yield, producing up to 32% more beans on treated plots compared with control plots. They also noticed increased nutrient uptake by beans as well as larger and heavier pods from electroculture systems.

Although this study provides some evidence to support the potential benefits of electroculture on bean production, it must be remembered that its results come from only one experiment and should be replicated elsewhere to verify their reliability.

Conclusion

Overall, scientific evidence for electroculture as an agricultural technique remains limited, and more in-depth studies need to be conducted to assess its potential benefits. Case studies provide some anecdotal support for potential gains through electroculture on plant growth and yield, however, more rigorous scientific tests need to be completed to verify these effects.

Electroculture may provide some advantages; however, it should not be seen as a replacement for effective agricultural practices like soil management, nutrient management, and integrated pest management - practices scientifically proven to enhance plant growth and yield and which should form the core of any agricultural management strategy.

Electroculture remains an unproven technique and more research needs to be conducted into its potential benefits and drawbacks.

CURRENT TRENDS IN ELECTROCULTURE

Electrostatic Precipitators (ESPs)

Electrostatic precipitators (ESPs) are devices designed to remove particulate matter (PM) from industrial exhaust gasses using electrostatic charges that attract and collect particles onto electrodes, before being mechanically extracted by mechanical means. ESP technology has long been employed in industries like power generation, cement production, and steel manufacturing; more recently researchers have begun exploring its use for agriculture purposes - specifically reducing PM concentration in greenhouses while simultaneously improving plant growth.

Studies have demonstrated the harmful effects of high levels of PM on plant growth, as it blocks sunlight and reduces photosynthetic activity. When combined with ESPs for greenhouse air purification, researchers observed increased plant growth and yield; additionally, using these filters can also help decrease plant disease transmission since many pathogens travel via PM.

However, using ESPs in agriculture presents several obstacles and drawbacks, including the high energy consumption necessary to operate them and prohibitive costs for installation and maintenance for smaller-scale farmers. Still, greenhouse growers may find ESPs an invaluable asset for improving plant health and yield.

Electrohydrodynamics

Electrohydrodynamics (EHD) is the study of interactions between electric fields and fluids. EHD technology has been employed across numerous fields, from aerospace engineering and biomedical engineering to microfluidics; researchers in agriculture have also explored its use to increase water distribution and uptake by plants.

One application of EHD in agriculture is electrohydrodynamic spraying, which involves using an electric field to generate a fine mist of liquid. Studies have proven EHD spraying is more efficient than traditional spraying methods because it offers uniform coverage while decreasing waste and cost. Furthermore, using this technology can significantly decrease water and pesticide requirements for crop treatment, providing cost savings as well as environmental advantages.

Electrohydrodynamic pumping is another potential application of EHD in agriculture that could use an electric field to move fluids. This technology could help enhance soil moisture distribution in regions with limited rainfall or poor-quality soil; however, more research needs to be conducted to establish its feasibility and effectiveness.

Electrically Conductive Polymers

Electrically Conductive Polymers (ECPs) are a type of material that boosts both electrical conductivity and mechanical flexibility, making them suitable for applications including sensors, actuators, energy storage devices, and agriculture research projects. Researchers have explored their use as soil monitors as well as plant health monitors.

ECPs could provide farmers with a solution for monitoring soil moisture. Researchers can embed ECPs in the soil to monitor changes in electrical conductivity that correspond with changes in moisture content - providing researchers with data for improved irrigation efficiency and reduced water usage.

ECPs also find use in agriculture as plant health sensors. By embedding ECPs into plant leaves, researchers can measure changes in electrical conductivity that correspond with changes in plant health - potentially helping detect early signs of stress or disease for timely intervention.

But there are also challenges associated with ECP use in agriculture. One such challenge is material degradation due to exposure in harsh agricultural environments; production costs may also be prohibitively expensive for large-scale applications; nonetheless, ECPs could prove an invaluable asset for farmers looking to monitor plant and soil health in real-time.

One challenge of electroculture technologies lies in their implementation cost; many require expensive specialized equipment and require expert knowledge for implementation, which may impede small-scale farmers from adopting such solutions due to a lack of capital for new equipment purchases.

The environmental impact of these technologies also poses a considerable hurdle, for example, the high energy consumption of ESPs could contribute to greenhouse gas emissions if their electricity comes from fossil fuel sources, while EHD spraying raises concerns regarding fine mist's effect on nearby ecosystems.

Electroculture holds great promise to transform agriculture in the coming years, by improving water distribution, nutrient uptake, and plant health monitoring technologies that could create more sustainable and efficient farming practices. Furthermore, its capacity to reduce PM levels could have significant health implications - particularly among farm workers exposed to high concentrations of PM regularly.

Electroculture is an exciting field with endless potential applications in agriculture. Current trends such as ESPs, EHDs, and ECPs demonstrate the variety of approaches being taken to enhance crop growth while decreasing environmental impact and increasing efficiency in farming operations. Unfortunately, electroculture still faces several barriers before its widespread adoption by farmers.

FUTURE TRENDS IN ELECTROCULTURE

Electrochemical sensors are devices that use electrochemical reactions to detect and quantify specific substances within a sample, making them useful in many different fields such as biomedical research, environmental monitoring, food safety monitoring, and agriculture. When used effectively they could assist with soil/water quality monitoring as well as pesticide detection or analysis of plant nutrients.

Electrochemical sensors offer another potential application in agriculture: monitoring pesticide levels in soil and water. Pesticides have serious negative impacts on both human health and the environment, making their detection crucial for food safety and sustainability. Electrochemical sensors have high sensitivities for detecting low levels of pesticides quickly - making them an excellent tool to track pesticide levels in agriculture.

Electrochemical sensors offer another potential application in agriculture: plant nutrient analysis. Nutrient deficiencies or imbalances can have major ramifications on crop yield and quality. Farmers using electrochemical sensors can measure concentrations of nutrients present in soil or plant tissues to adjust fertilization practices accordingly for maximum crop growth.

However, electrochemical sensors still present some difficulties for use in agriculture. One difficulty involves creating sensors that specifically target analyte concentration and can operate across complex sample matrices; another need involves low-cost portable sensors which can be easily utilized by farmers without the need for special training.

Electroosmotic Flow

Electroosmotic flow (EOF) refers to the movement of liquid through porous materials under an electric field. It has applications in many fields such as microfluidics and separation science; agriculture may use it to improve irrigation efficiency, nutrient uptake, and soil remediation.

One application of electroosmotic farming technology in agriculture could include using electroosmotic pumps to deliver water and nutrients directly to plant roots. Electroosmotic pumps can move fluids through porous media with extreme precision, enabling targeted delivery of water and nutrients directly to root zones - potentially cutting back on water usage and fertilizer waste, leading to greater crop yields while lessening environmental impact.

Electroosmotic remediation technology could also play an integral role in agriculture by remediating soil. Electroosmotic remediation works by employing an electric field to transport contaminants out of the soil and remove them, making this approach cost-effective and environmentally friendly, eliminating costly excavation methods or disruptive disposal methods.

However, electroosmotic remediation in agriculture still presents several obstacles and challenges. One issue lies with optimizing the electroosmotic pump design to maximize high flow rates and long-term stability, and there is also a need for further research regarding its environmental impacts on soil microbial communities.

Electromagnetic Fields

Electromagnetic fields (EMFs) are an energy form resulting from the interaction between electric and magnetic fields, used to improve medical imaging and communications; as well as agricultural uses including improving plant growth, soil quality, and pest management.

One potential application of EMFs in agriculture is magnetic fields to stimulate plant growth. Studies have demonstrated how magnetic fields can increase plant growth, seed germination, and nutrient uptake across multiple crops - leading to improved crop yields while simultaneously decreasing synthetic fertilizer use, leading to more sustainable farming practices.

EMFs in agriculture may also prove useful as a pest management strategy by employing magnetic fields for repelling insect pests, thus decreasing pesticide usage while simultaneously encouraging more eco-friendly management practices.

Electric fields present another potential application of EMFs in agriculture: soil remediation. Electric fields have been employed to increase bioremediation of polluted soils by stimulating microorganism growth that breaks down pollutants; this technology may enable cost-effective and environmentally friendly remediation solutions, thus eliminating costly excavation or disposal methods.

However, EMFs still present several challenges for agriculture. One such difficulty lies in optimizing magnetic field strength and duration to achieve the desired impact on plant growth and pest management. Furthermore, additional research must be conducted on potential EMF impacts on soil microbial communities as well as non-target organisms.

In conclusion, Electroculture is an emerging field with numerous promising applications in agriculture. Electrochemical sensors, EOF, and EMF technologies are among the many that are being tested to increase crop growth while decreasing environmental impact and improving farming efficiency. While electroculture remains challenging at times, its potential benefits make it a worthwhile area of research to address to advance sustainability and productivity within agriculture.

APPLICATIONS OF ELECTROCULTURE

Crop Growth Enhancement

Electroculture holds the potential to enhance crop growth and yield through various mechanisms, including enhanced nutrient uptake, water use efficiency, and photosynthesis. One form of electroculture technology used to accelerate plant growth is an electrostatic precipitator (ESP). These devices use an electric field to capture particulate matter in the air; when used for agriculture they help reduce dust in feedlots thereby improving respiratory health and decreasing risks for respiratory infections.

Electrohydrodynamics (EHD), another electroculture technology used to boost crop growth, involves applying an electric field to fluids to induce fluid flows and other phenomena. EHD has been successfully employed to enhance water and nutrient distribution, leading to greater crop growth and yield. Furthermore, its application improves irrigation system efficiencies while decreasing water usage thereby improving crop water use efficiency.

Electrically Conductive Polymers (ECPs) are another promising electroculture technology with the potential to accelerate crop growth. ECPs are flexible materials capable of conducting electricity while remaining lightweight; ECPs have been utilized by farmers in agriculture as flexible electrodes integrated into plant leaves or roots to monitor plant activity while providing electrical stimulation that boosts photosynthesis and nutrient uptake.

Soil Remediation

Soil contamination is a serious environmental concern that has the potential to negatively impact human health, wildlife, and the environment. Electroculture technology offers one solution to remediate polluted soils cost-effectively and sustainably: Electrokinetics. Electrokinetics involves applying an electric field directly onto soil surface layers which draws contaminants towards electrodes; then these contaminants can be safely extracted from the soil and removed for disposal.

Electroculture technology used for soil remediation includes electrochemical treatment of polluted soil. Electrochemical treatments utilize an electric current to break down contaminants into less toxic compounds or elements; it has been effectively employed in remediating heavy metal-contaminated, organic compound-rich, and pollutant-saturated environments.

Pest Control

Agriculture poses a complex pest management challenge that has the potential to have negative consequences for crop yield and quality as well as human and environmental health. Electroculture may offer more eco-friendly methods of pest control such as electromagnetic fields (EMFs) to repel insect pests from entering crop fields or creating zones within fields where EMFs repel insect pests. EMFs have been employed successfully against insects.

Electroculture technology that has been employed for pest control includes electrostatic sprayers. Electrostatic sprayers use an electric charge to generate a fine mist of pesticide that attracts plant surfaces, providing a more targeted application of the substance and potentially decreasing pesticide usage while increasing efficacy measures.

In conclusion, Electroculture technology holds great promise to improve agriculture, including crop growth, soil remediation, and pest control. Although there remain challenges that must be met before fully realizing its potential benefits for agricultural production. Researching electroculture technologies represents an exciting avenue of investigation to increase sustainability and productivity within farming operations.

PART 7: PRACTICAL ASPECTS OF ELECTROCULTURE

Electroculture is an interesting subject because it combines elements from multiple disciplines - physics, chemistry, biology, and agriculture - in its practice. Here we will look at its practical aspects such as electrode selection, power source, frequency/voltage settings, timing considerations, safety issues, environmental considerations, and costs associated with electroculture systems.

Electrode Selection

Selecting suitable electrodes for electroculture is crucial to its success. Electrodes deliver electrical energy directly to plants, so they must withstand moisture and acidity conditions of soil conditions - copper, aluminum, and graphite are popular choices as electrodes.

Copper is an excellent conductor of electricity and is highly resistant to corrosion. Furthermore, it is relatively affordable and widely accessible; therefore copper electrodes are widely used in electroculture operations with smaller operations.

Aluminum electrodes are another popular choice, due to their being lightweight, durable, and corrosion-resistant. Aluminum electrodes tend to be preferred over copper for larger operations because of their higher cost.

Graphite electrodes are an ideal choice, as it acts as a natural conductor of electricity and chemically stable material. Although more expensive than copper and aluminum electrodes, graphite may produce superior results.

The choice of electrode depends on the specific needs and conditions of the crop being grown and soil conditions. Generally speaking, however, electrodes should be constructed from materials that resist corrosion while effectively conducting electricity.

Power Source

Electroculture requires a reliable power source that can reliably provide electricity to electrodes. There are various options for such sources such as batteries, solar panels, or generators available to choose from.

Batteries are an attractive solution for smaller businesses because they're portable and relatively affordable, yet limited capacity requires regular recharging sessions.

Solar panels make an excellent option for electroculture because they provide a steady supply of electricity without needing a generator or grid connection. Plus, solar panels are environmentally-friendly and long-lived! However, larger operations may find solar installations costly.

Generators are an excellent solution for larger operations as they offer high levels of power output. Unfortunately, however, they are noisy, produce emissions, and require routine maintenance to operate optimally.

Depending on the size and nature of your operation, selecting an ideal power source depends on both availability of electricity as well as reliability. Electroculture requires reliable electricity supply sources that are consistent.

Frequency And Voltage

Electroculture requires specific frequencies and voltages depending on the specific crop and soil conditions; different crops need different frequencies/voltages for optimal growth.

Typically, a frequency and voltage combination of 50-60 Hz and 1-5 volts should be suitable for most crops; however, these settings may need to be modified depending on your particular crop and soil conditions.

As an example, crops grown in sandy soil may require a higher voltage than crops in clay soil; similarly, crops that are sensitive to electrical stimulation may need lower frequencies and voltage.

The frequency and voltage of electrical signals can be adjusted using a transformer or electronic device that can be programmed to deliver specific frequencies and voltage levels to electrodes.

Timing

The electrical stimulation should take place during the growth phase of a plant's development; its frequency and duration should be adjusted based on this stage of its life.

At first, plants may require shorter and less frequent electrical pulses; as they develop and grow larger, this stimulation may become more frequent and powerful.

The timing of electrical stimulation also depends on the specific crop being grown; some require it throughout their entire growth cycle while other crops only need it during specific stages.

The electrical stimulation should generally take place either early morning or late evening when temperatures and humidity levels are at their lowest to reduce the risk of an electrical discharge that could harm plants.

Safety

Safety when conducting electroculture should always be of primary concern, as improper electrical stimulation could prove harmful both to plants and humans alike.

For optimal safety, high-quality electrodes and an uninterrupted power source must be utilized. Furthermore, electrical equipment should be regularly checked and maintained to avoid accidents from occurring.

Safety guidelines must always be strictly observed when handling electrical equipment, and this includes wearing protective gear such as gloves and glasses while following proper procedures for handling such products.

Ecological Considerations

Environmentalism should always be kept in mind when using electroculture. Electric energy can have detrimental effects on air and water quality, leading to adverse consequences that require careful consideration when using electric energy for electroculture purposes.

To reduce our environmental impact, it is vitally important to use renewable power sources like solar panels or wind turbines as sources of power. Furthermore, proper disposal procedures must be observed when disposing of electrical equipment or batteries.

Cost

Electroculture's cost varies significantly based on several factors, including operation size, electrode type, and power source; generally speaking, electroculture tends to be more costly than traditional farming techniques.

However, higher yield and improved plant health may offset some of the upfront costs of electroculture. Furthermore, using renewable energy sources like solar panels may further lower the long-term costs of electroculture.

Conclusion

Electroculture is a promising field of agriculture with the potential to significantly enhance plant growth, health, and yield. To be effective, electroculture requires high-quality electrodes connected to an efficient power source with appropriate timing and frequency of electrical stimulation.

Safety and environmental considerations must also be kept in mind when employing electroculture. While electroculture may be more costly than traditional farming techniques, its potential advantages such as higher yield and improved plant health could make it a worthwhile investment for farmers.

IMPLEMENTING ELECTROCULTURE IN PRACTICE

Implementing electroculture requires special tools, including electrodes and controllers, as well as specific protocols. Electroculture involves passing a low-voltage electrical current through soil, seeds, or plants in a controlled fashion to achieve beneficial effects.

Step one in electroculture implementation is choosing the appropriate equipment. Farmers can select from a selection of electrodes and controllers tailored to the size and nature of their operation; electrodes may be either buried in the soil or attached directly to plants for easier deployment; controllers regulate electrical current levels to provide different levels of stimulation depending on where your plants are in their growth cycles.

Once they have chosen equipment, farmers need to prepare both soil and plants for electroculture. Soil should be moist but not waterlogged, while plants should be healthy without pests or diseases. Furthermore, farmers must make sure the electrodes are correctly placed within contact with either soil or plants.

Farmers must be vigilant during electroculture processes to monitor electrical current levels and make adjustments as needed, monitor plant health and growth, and make any required modifications to the frequency or duration of electric current.

Factors Affecting The Effectiveness Of Electroculture

Electroculture's effectiveness may depend on many variables, including the crops grown, soil type, and environmental conditions. Research suggests it works better on sandy soils than clay ones; furthermore, certain crops, such as tomatoes, may respond more favorably than others to electroculture treatment.

Environmental conditions like temperature and humidity can also influence the effectiveness of electroculture. Electroculture works best under warmer, humid environments as this stimulates microorganism growth in the soil. Nonetheless, electroculture is still effective under other circumstances, and farmers should experiment with various settings until they find what works best for their operation.

Electroculture success also hinges on the duration and frequency of its electrical current. While higher frequencies and longer durations may result in faster plant growth and yield, too much stimulation could cause damage or reduce production.

Challenges And Limitations Of Electroculture

Though electroculture has produced encouraging results in various experiments, its implementation remains subject to certain obstacles and restrictions. One such obstacle is its high equipment cost requirements - this may make adopting it challenging for small-scale farmers.

One limitation of electroculture is its limited scientific data on its long-term effects on soil health and plant growth. While studies on its short-term impacts exist, more research must be conducted to ascertain its long-term consequences on both.

Electroculture may not be suitable for all crops and soil types; therefore, farmers must conduct tests to assess its effectiveness for their specific operation, making adjustments as necessary.

Conclusion

Electroculture is an innovative farming technique with great promise in agricultural settings, offering great potential to increase crop yields while simultaneously decreasing chemical fertilizers and pesticide usage, improving soil health, and strengthening resistance against pests and diseases. Implementation is still in its early stages, yet farmers can benefit from using this technique by selecting suitable equipment, properly preparing soil and plants, and monitoring the growth and health of their plants. But there are still challenges and limitations associated with electroculture; farmers should conduct tests to determine its suitability for their specific operation. Through further research and development, electroculture could become an economical and sustainable agricultural technique for farmers.

BEST PRACTICES FOR ELECTROCULTURE

Implementation of electroculture requires careful planning, preparation, and monitoring to achieve maximum benefits for farmers. Here, we discuss some best practices of electroculture to maximize its use in practice.

Select The Appropriate Equipment

Step one in successfully implementing electroculture is selecting suitable equipment. This may include an electrical generator, electrodes, and wires specifically designed to facilitate electroculture for maximum results and safety. When selecting equipment to facilitate this type of work high-quality devices specifically tailored towards electroculture must be utilized to ensure its safe implementation and optimal results.

Farmers should carefully consider the voltage, current, frequency, and duration of electrical current. While higher voltages and frequencies can lead to faster growth and greater yields, they also increase the risk of plant damage - finding the balance between stimulating plant growth and protecting its health is vitally important.

Prepare The Soil

Before embarking on electroculture, farmers must properly prepare the soil to optimize plant growth. This means testing its pH level, nutrient levels, and organic matter content - optimal results being found with soils with a pH range between 6.0-7.5 with high organic matter content.

Agricultural lime and sulfur should be added as necessary to correct soil pH imbalances, while compost, manure, or cover crops should also be utilized to improve structure and nutrient availability in their soils.

Farmers Should Prepare The Plants

Farmers must also prepare the plants for electroculture. This involves selecting suitable crops and planting them at an optimal time; electroculture works best on crops sensitive to electrical currents, such as tomatoes, peppers, and cucumbers.

Farmers must ensure their plants are free from pests and diseases before initiating electroculture to prevent further damage or reduced growth due to plant stress.

Monitor The Electrical Current

Farmers should monitor the electrical current during electroculture to ensure it is applied appropriately and does not damage plants. They should also make sure electrodes do not come into contact with plants.

Farmers conducting electroculture should pay particular attention to temperature and humidity levels during electroculture as these can significantly impact its effectiveness. Maintaining ideal environmental conditions will encourage beneficial microorganisms to flourish in their soil environment.

Monitor The Growth And Health Of Plants

Farmers should monitor the development and health of plants during electroculture to ensure they respond positively. This involves taking measurements such as plant height, leaf size, stem diameter, color assessment, and overall plant health assessment.

If electroculture fails to satisfy plants, farmers may need to adjust the voltage, frequency, or duration of electrical current as well as experiment with different crops or soil types.

Conclusion

Electroculture is an exciting agricultural technique with great promise, as it has the power to increase crop yields while simultaneously decreasing chemical fertilizers and pesticide use, improving soil health, and helping farmers meet sustainable economic goals. But its implementation requires careful planning, preparation, and monitoring to achieve the best results; farmers should select suitable equipment, prepare the soil properly before planting any seedlings, and monitor electrical current and environmental conditions as well as plant growth and health for maximum effectiveness if this technique is to become an affordable sustainable practice for them.

COST-BENEFIT ANALYSIS OF ELECTROCULTURE

Electroculture has shown promising results in laboratory experiments and field trials, but more work needs to be done on its economic viability and feasibility. Cost-benefit analysis provides a useful way of examining these costs and benefits of electroculture implementation, helping farmers and policymakers make more informed decisions regarding its implementation.

COSTS OF ELECTROCULTURE

Equipment Costs

Electroculture's main cost component is its equipment requirements: an electrical generator, electrodes, and wires. The exact costs depend on the size and type of system chosen - typically from $5,000-$20,000 per acre on average - making widespread adoption of electroculture more challenging than anticipated.

Installation And Maintenance Costs

Electroculture involves not only equipment costs but also installation and maintenance fees for its installation and ongoing upkeep. Farmers will have to hire experts to install the system and provide ongoing maintenance to keep it working optimally - typically costing anywhere between $1,000 to $10,000 per acre per year; installation and maintenance expenses may present barriers for smaller-scale farmers who lack resources available to hire experts for installation/upkeep duties.

Training And Education Costs

Electroculture's additional costs involve training and education expenses for farmers and agricultural workers who are new to managing electroculture systems, including workshops and programs as well as hiring experts for guidance and support - this can range anywhere from $500-5,000 per acre depending on its complexity. Proper education about electroculture use ensures its maximum benefits are realized.

QUANTIFYING COSTS AND BENEFITS

Methods For Quantifying Costs And Benefits

There are various techniques for quantifying the costs and benefits associated with electroculture farming operations, including net present value analysis, cost-benefit analysis, and return on investment analysis. Each method offers its own set of strengths and weaknesses; ultimately the choice will depend on both your specific farming operation's circumstances and goals for analysis.

Case Studies of Electroculture Implementation

Numerous case studies have been undertaken to analyze the costs and benefits of electroculture in practice. One such research project conducted in Spain demonstrated how using electroculture for tomato production led to an estimated net present value of EUR8,803 per hectare versus a net present value of EUR5,304 with conventional farming methods; similarly, in India, electroculture generated a net present value of Rs 54,029 per acre when compared with Rs 43,395 using conventional farming techniques.

Comparison With Traditional Farming Methods

Comparing the costs and benefits of electroculture farming methods to those associated with traditional farming can provide an accurate picture of their economic impact. A US study concluded that electroculture proved more profitable than traditional farming methods for growing corn, as it increased yields by 23% with an estimated net present value per acre of $5,462 as compared with $3882 with traditional methods.

NET PRESENT VALUE ANALYSIS

Calculation Of Net Present Value

Net present value analysis is an increasingly popular means of evaluating the economic viability of electroculture. The net present value measures the difference between the present value of anticipated benefits and the present value of expected costs over an agreed-upon time frame, typically by taking these steps:

Estimate the expected costs and benefits of electroculture over an expected period (typically 5-10 years).

Calculate the present value of anticipated costs and benefits using a discount rate that accounts for the time value of money.

Subtract the present value of expected costs from that of expected benefits to find the net present value.

Discount Rate And Sensitivity Analysis

The choice of discount rate can have a dramatic impact on the results of net present value analysis. A higher discount rate will lead to lower net present values while lower ones lead to greater ones. A sensitivity analysis can be performed to assess their respective impacts on the results of the analysis.

Interpretation Of Results

Electroculture's net present value can be used to measure its economic viability and feasibility. A positive net present value signifies that anticipated benefits exceed anticipated costs; conversely, negative net present values indicate just the opposite. Furthermore, its magnitude can also help compare its economic impact with traditional farming techniques or technologies.

COST-BENEFIT ANALYSIS

When considering electroculture as an investment option, many variables must be taken into consideration, including equipment cost, power requirements for running the system, and potential increases in crop yield and quality. The analysis will vary based on these elements.

Benefits:

- Increased Crop Yields: Studies suggest that electroculture can significantly boost crop yields by as much as 30% or more, providing farmers with increased profits and helping meet growing food demands.

- Improved Plant Quality: Electrical stimulation can greatly enhance plant quality and health, increasing resistance against diseases and pests while simultaneously increasing nutritional value.

- Reduced Water Usage: Proponents of electroculture have suggested that it can reduce water usage by up to 50% - something which would prove especially helpful in drought-prone regions.

- Reduced Fertilizer and Pesticide Usage: Electroculture can potentially help plants be more resistant to pests and diseases, decreasing their need for chemical fertilizers and pesticides - something which could be good for the environment.

Costs:

- Initial Investment: For farmers considering electroculture technology, initial costs can be high and farmers will likely need to make significant initial investments before embarking on this path.

- Energy Use: Electroculture systems rely on a constant electricity supply for operation, which may be expensive and contribute to carbon emissions.

- Maintenance costs: Electroculture systems need periodic upkeep and repair work to stay functional, which adds another expense to its total price.

- Lack of Scientific Evidence: While studies have provided encouraging results, scientific proof for electroculture remains limited and this uncertainty could make some farmers reluctant to invest in its technology.

In conclusion, Electroculture holds great promise to increase crop yields, enhance plant quality and decrease water and chemical input usage; however, its high initial investment costs, ongoing maintenance expenses, and energy consumption requirements must also be carefully considered before proceeding with the operation. A cost-benefit analysis tailored specifically to each farming operation would help determine whether electroculture is indeed a viable option for increasing agricultural productivity.

RETURN ON INVESTMENT ANALYSIS

Conducting a return on investment (ROI) analysis for electroculture allows farmers to gauge whether or not its benefits outweigh its costs, providing a clear understanding of financial implications related to investing in electroculture technology and enabling informed decisions regarding whether or not to adopt it.

Here are a few reasons why conducting an ROI analysis on electroculture is necessary:

- Establish the Financial Feasibility of Electroculture: Adopting electroculture technology can be expensive. A return on investment (ROI) analysis helps farmers assess whether its potential advantages - increased yields, better plants, reduced water usage and chemical input costs, etc - make adopting electroculture worth its initial investment and ongoing operational expenses.

- Identification of Risks and Uncertainties: Conducting an ROI analysis requires making assumptions regarding potential benefits and costs associated with electroculture, to help farmers identify potential risks and uncertainties that could reduce its financial viability - for instance, if yield assumptions are unrealistically optimistic, ROI of electroculture may be lower than anticipated.

- Assess Payback Period: To assess payback periods is to conduct an ROI analysis on their electroculture investments to ascertain when their benefits outweigh costs, which is essential in establishing their financial viability and determining the financial feasibility of investments like this one.

- Compare Electroculture ROI With Other Investments: Farmers must make careful choices with limited resources when it comes to their investments, such as purchasing equipment or investing in different crops. A return-on-investment (ROI) analysis allows farmers to compare potential returns of electroculture against similar investments such as purchasing new machinery.

In conclusion, conducting a return on investment analysis for electroculture is vitally important to enable farmers to make informed decisions regarding whether to adopt this technology or not. An ROI analysis helps evaluate financial feasibility, identify risks and uncertainties, and compare potential returns between investments like electroculture.

Estimate The Potential Increase In Revenue And Profitability From Higher Yields

Electroculture may lead to higher crop yields and profitability for farmers. More produce means increased revenues. Furthermore, improved quality could allow higher prices to be charged at sales events for crops grown using electroculture techniques resulting in even greater profit gains for these farms.

Electroculture's effects on revenue and profitability depend on many variables, including crop type, market demand for it, and overall costs associated with farming operations. Farmers will need to conduct a return on investment analysis to estimate any potential increases in revenues and profitability related to electroculture that might apply specifically to them.

ROI Calculation

Determining the return on investment (ROI) of electroculture requires several key financial metrics, including payback period, net present value (NPV), and internal rate of return (IRR). Here is how each of these can be calculated:

- Payback Period: To calculate a payback period in electroculture, divide the initial investment in terms of annual cash inflows generated. For example, if an initial investment of $50,000 and annual cash flows totaling $10,000 were involved, five years would pass before paying back any part of your initial investment.

- Net Present Value (NPV): To calculate electroculture's net present value (NPV), first estimate its expected cash inflows and outflows over its life, and then discount those cash flows back to present value using an appropriate discount rate. If its resulting NPV is positive then its expected returns exceed its required rate of return; conversely, if its resultant negative NPV indicates less return than anticipated by investors.

- Internal Rate of Return (IRR): To calculate IRR in electroculture, use trial-and-error to find the discount rate that renders its net present value equal to zero and represents the expected rate of return over its lifespan. When using trial-and-error methods to estimate the IRR of investment in electroculture.

Electroculture investment returns vary significantly based on your farming operation's unique circumstances, taking into account factors like equipment costs, expected yield increases, and market demand for crops - these all play a factor.

In conclusion, to calculate the Return On Investment of electroculture farming, farmers need to evaluate its payback period, net present value, and internal rate of return of the investment. These metrics serve as a framework for assessing the financial feasibility of adopting this technology and making an informed decision on whether or not to invest in electroculture.

Sensitivity Analysis

Sensitivity analysis is an essential step when evaluating the return on investment (ROI) potential of electroculture, as it allows farmers to determine how changes to key assumptions and variables could alter its profitability. When conducting such an evaluation for electroculture investments, farmers must bear in mind the following considerations when conducting an analysis:

- Yield Improvements: One of the key assumptions used in an ROI analysis of electroculture is expected increases in crop yield. If actual yield improvements fall below expectations, the return on investment will be lower than anticipated; conversely, if they exceed them, ROI could increase considerably.

- Market Prices: Changes in market prices for crops can have a direct effect on the Return On Investment in Electroculture. While higher prices could lead to greater profitability, lower ones could diminish it significantly and impact ROI significantly.

- Input Costs: Input costs such as electricity can have an enormous effect on the profitability of electroculture. If these expenses exceed expectations, their impact will diminish and return-on-investment will decrease accordingly.

- Maintenance And Repair Costs: Maintenance and repair expenses related to electroculture equipment can also have a dramatic effect on return on investment (ROI). If these costs exceed expectations, this could decrease substantially and decrease ROI significantly.

- Uncertainties: Electroculture involves various uncertainties and risks that can compromise its return on investment, such as unpredictable weather patterns, pests, and diseases, changes to regulations or policies, etc.

To address these risks and uncertainties, farmers must conduct a sensitivity analysis that analyzes how changes to key assumptions and variables could alter electroculture's return on investment. Such an evaluation can identify any potential risks while providing insight into ways they may be mitigated or avoided altogether - for instance investing in crop insurance can help to minimize risks associated with any single crop.

Overall, sensitivity analysis is an integral component of assessing the potential return on investment (ROI) of electroculture. By understanding how changes to key assumptions and variables could alter profitability, farmers can make informed decisions regarding whether or not to invest in electroculture as well as develop plans to limit risks and uncertainties associated with it.

Conclusion

Based on the Return On Investment analysis for electroculture, it is evident that investing in this technology could yield benefits. Increases in crop yield and revenue could provide farmers with a positive Return On Investment return - making electroculture an attractive investment choice.

Payback period, net present value (NPV), and internal rate of return (IRR) are key metrics that indicate whether investing in electroculture is feasible. Sensitivity analysis helps reveal how changes to key assumptions or variables could alter profitability; risks related to electroculture should also be evaluated to develop appropriate mitigation strategies against its risks.

Given all this, my advice to farmers would be to conduct an in-depth examination of their farming operation and consider the possible impacts of electroculture on yields and profitability. If their analysis shows electroculture as a viable option, farmers must then carefully weigh costs, benefits, and risks before investing in this technology. A return-on-investment analysis indicates that electroculture could prove a profitable investment option if managed responsibly by those willing to accept the risks associated with its adoption.

CONCLUSION

Plants are electrochemical organisms capable of producing and responding to electrical signals through physiological processes such as the movement of ions across cell membranes or the release of chemicals by plant cells. These electrical signals play an integral role in various functions such as growth, development, and stress responses in plants.

Electroculture involves applying low-voltage, high-frequency electric charges to plants, soil, and water sources to stimulate plant growth and resistance against pests and diseases. This technology relies on the principle that plants absorb energy from electrical fields which may help increase their growth potential and protect them against potential infestation.

Electroculture can help increase crop yields while decreasing pesticide and fertilizer use and improving soil quality. By applying an electrical charge to the soil, electroculture stimulates beneficial microorganisms that promote plant growth while protecting against pathogens that could threaten it.

Electroculture in horticulture can aid the growth of ornamental plants, fruits, and vegetables by applying controlled electrical charges directly to them. By doing so, electroculture can increase growth rate, and resistance against pests/diseases, and boost nutrient uptake of these species.

Electroculture can dramatically enhance grape quality and wine production. By applying an electrical charge to vines, electroculture stimulates root growth and increased water absorption capacity resulting in higher yields with improved grape quality and yields.

Electroculture can enhance both Aquaponics and hydroponics systems by applying an electrical charge to the water, increasing oxygenation levels, nutrient uptake by plants, and stimulating beneficial bacteria for fish health.

Electroculture in forestry can promote tree growth while improving resistance against pests and diseases. By applying an electrical charge directly to both soil and trees, electroculture can increase their nutrient uptake and stimulate their growth; creating healthier forests.

Electroculture's primary principle rests upon the idea that applying electrical current and voltage directly to plants can stimulate their production and transmission of electrical signals, leading to improved plant growth and health. Studies have also demonstrated how electrical stimulation increases plant uptake of nutrients for increased yields and better agricultural products.

Electroculture utilizes another key principle known as electro-osmosis to move water and nutrients through the soil as a result of electrical forces. When an electric field is applied to soil, charged particles attract electrodes which cause changes to a soil structure that lead to increased movement of water and nutrients towards plant roots, improving soil health as well as availability resulting in greater plant growth and yield.

Electroculture's theoretical foundations also involve understanding the role of electrical signaling in plant stress response. When plants encounter different kinds of stresses such as drought, disease, or pest infestations, their bodies produce electrical signals which initiate physiological reactions aimed at mitigating any damage done by such stressors. By applying electrical current and voltage directly to plants during electroculture sessions, electroculture aims to enhance these stress responses for improved plant resilience and health.

One of the key advantages of electroculture is its potential to increase crop yields and quality. Studies have revealed that electroculture can stimulate root system growth, increase the absorption of nutrients and water, enhance photosynthesis, and lead to greater yields from crops. Furthermore, electroculture may enhance the nutritional content of crops making them more suitable for human consumption.

Electroculture's other advantage lies in its potential to reduce chemical fertilizers and pesticide usage. Traditional farming practices rely heavily on their use, leading to environmental impacts like soil degradation, water pollution, harm to beneficial insects, wildlife, and even beneficial insects being killed off. By improving plant health resilience through electroculture farming becomes more sustainable and environmentally friendly.

Electroculture can enhance soil health by stimulating microorganism activity and encouraging soil aeration. Electrical currents stimulate microbial activity within the soil, leading to improved nutrient cycling and structure development that contribute to greater water retention, decreased erosion rates, and overall improved soil health overall.

Electroculture offers more than just advantages to plant growth and soil health; it may also reduce greenhouse gas emissions. Traditional farming practices produce carbon dioxide, methane, and nitrous oxide emissions; by decreasing chemical input requirements and improving soil health through electroculture practices it may help offset these emissions to address climate change efforts.

Electroculture may offer some significant benefits, yet its implementation must also be conducted safely to protect human health and safety. Electrical currents can pose potential threats to our well-being; to ensure safe implementation of electroculture. Furthermore, some experts remain skeptical of its efficacy; therefore further study must be conducted into both its strengths and limitations to fully comprehend it.

Electroculture faces numerous obstacles, such as safety concerns, controversial discussions, doubts among members, technical and economic challenges, and policy implications.

One of the major safety risks associated with electroculture is electric shock. Electrical currents can be harmful to human health and safety, so appropriate precautions must be taken to implement electroculture safely. Farmers and workers must receive training on how to handle electrical equipment safely as well as properly grounding systems to avoid electric shock incidents.

Electroculture continues to face some controversy and skepticism from critics; critics assert its benefits aren't supported by scientific data while others question its practicality and scalability. Further research must be conducted to fully comprehend its capabilities and limitations as well as address these concerns.

Technical and economic obstacles stand in the way of electroculture's widespread adoption. Equipment costs for small-scale farmers may be prohibitively costly; additionally, this technology needs a reliable electricity source that may not always be readily available; technical challenges include needing expert services to design and install systems as well as ongoing maintenance to maintain optimal performance;

Electroculture's future looks bright despite these obstacles, with ongoing research and development likely leading to technological breakthroughs and novel applications of electroculture in various settings. With global population numbers continuing to expand and food demand increasing at an ever-increasing pace, electroculture will become even more critical as a sustainable farming method to meet these demands while minimizing environmental damage.

Policy implications of electroculture should also be carefully considered. Regulatory frameworks must be put in place to ensure safe and responsible implementation as well as address potential environmental or health impacts; furthermore, policies promoting research and development as well as providing incentives for farmers adopting electroculture may help increase the widespread adoption of this technology.

Electroculture holds tremendous promise to revolutionize multiple fields; however, its successful implementation in practice will require careful attention to practical considerations, including developing effective adoption and integration strategies into existing agricultural and horticultural practices.

Electroculture technology must be implemented properly in practice, which involves developing appropriate equipment and infrastructure for applying current and voltage to plants as well as training farmers and growers in its use. Furthermore, effective strategies must be devised for integrating electroculture into existing agricultural or horticultural practices taking into account factors like crop type, soil conditions, and climate.

Another crucial practical consideration in electroculture is developing best practices. This requires identifying optimal parameters for electrical current and voltage as well as finding suitable electrodes and power sources for different crops and growing conditions. Furthermore, monitoring and control systems must also be put in place to ensure the safe application of electroculture.

An electroculture cost-benefit analysis will also be essential to its successful implementation in practice. While electroculture has the potential to boost plant growth and yield, reduce fertilizers use, improve soil health, and decrease fertilizer costs significantly, it must also take into account all costs related to setting up and operating an electroculture system - including equipment costs, labor expenses, and potential yield increases - when making this determination.

In conclusion, Electroculture offers an exciting way to enhance plant growth, yields, and health. While still an emerging technology with certain challenges and limitations, its potential lies within agriculture and horticulture in general. With continued research and development in this field, electroculture promises new applications that benefit both plants and the environment alike.

Manufactured by Amazon.ca
Acheson, AB